SEARCHING FOR SECURITY

Human security is a development buzzword of the 1990s. To attain security people need to feel safe from natural disasters, such as drought, and 'man-made' problems, such as unemployment. Women are a particularly insecure section of society with the impact of deprivation disproportionately shouldered by women throughout the developing world.

Searching for Security examines how economic, political and environmental factors have contributed to increased gender insecurity in the last decade. Analysing the impacts of insecurity induced by global changes on the lives of women throughout the developing world, the book discusses women's responses to these changing circumstances from Africa to Malaysia, and Hungary to the Caribbean.

By examining both the causes of insecurity and the gendered responses to it, this collection of essays makes a timely contribution to emerging policy efforts to recognise and address the issue of gender insecurity.

Isa Baud is Associate Professor at the Institute of Human Geography, University of Amsterdam.
Ines Smyth has recently joined OXFAM as a Policy Adviser.

ROUTLEDGE STUDIES IN DEVELOPMENT AND SOCIETY

1
SEARCHING FOR SECURITY
Women's Responses to Economic Transformations
Edited by Isa Baud and Ines Smyth

SEARCHING FOR SECURITY

Women's Responses to Economic Transformations

Edited by Isa Baud and Ines Smyth

London and New York

First published 1997
by Routledge
11 New Fetter Lane, London EC4P 4EE

Simultaneously published in the USA and Canada
by Routledge
29 West 35th Street, New York, NY 10001

Typeset in Garamond by Routledge
Printed and bound in Great Britain by Redwood Books,
Trowbridge, Wiltshire

British Library Cataloguing in Publication Data
A catalogue record for this book is available from the British Library

Library of Congress Cataloguing in Publication Data
Searching for security: women's responses to economic transformations/
edited by Isa Baud and Ines Smyth.
p. cm. – (Routledge studies in development & society)
Includes index.
1. Women – Developing countries – Economic conditions. 2. Women in
development – Developing countries. 3. Economic security – Developing
countries. I. Baud, I. S. A. II. Smyth, Ines, 1948 –
III. Series.
HQ1381. S45 1997   96-21815
305.42'091724–dc20   CIP

ISBN 0–415–14227–X

To the memory of Rita

CONTENTS

CONTENTS

CONTRIBUTORS

Maria Adamik is currently Research Associate in the Department of Social Policy, Institute of Social Policy of the Eotvos Lorant University in Budapest. Her main research interests are the impact of social policy on women and children, as well as the broader issues of gender and knowledge. She is involved in the Hungarian Ombudswoman Project, which is setting up an institute for women-friendly socio-legal services for women.

Isa Baud is Associate Professor at the Institute of Human Geography at the University of Amsterdam in the Netherlands. She is interested in issues of gender and development, focusing particularly on employment and industrialisation. Recent publications include *Gender, Small Scale Industry and Development Policy* (with G. A. de Bruijne, 1993, London: Intermediate Technology Publications), an article on new forms of trade union organisation and women in informal economic activities (1994), and *Solid Waste Management: Modes, Assessments, Appraisals and Linkages in Bangalore* (with H. Schenk), a book on urban informal recycling activities.

Jo Beall is a Lecturer in the Department of Social Policy and Administration at the London School of Economics. Her research interests cover gender and social policy, urban poverty, gender and development and participatory development. Publications include 'The Gender Dimensions of Urbanization and Urban Poverty', a paper presented at the INSTRAW/DAW Seminar on Women in Urban Areas (1993), and 'Integrating the Gender Variable into Urban Development:A Conceptual and Operational Framework',a paper prepared for the Development Assistance Committee of the OECD 1992.

Mayra Buvinić is a founding member and President of the International Center for Research on Women (ICRW). Under her leadership, ICRW has produced some of the seminal research and policy analysis of the last two decades, on women's economic conditions and women's health. Dr Buvinić's 'Projects for Women: Explaining their Misbehaviour' (*World Development*, 1988, vol. 14, no. 5, pp. 653–664) provided the first critical analysis of projects designed for women. She has written numerous papers on women and poverty, including a monograph – *Women, Poverty and Progress in the Third World* – for the *Headline Series* of the Foreign Policy Association. Her most recent work has focused on the relationships between adolescent motherhood, female headship and the reproduction of poverty in mother–child pairs.

Geeta Rao Gupta is Vice President of the International Center for Research on Women, and works on the Center's reproductive health projects, including the Women and AIDS Research Program. Dr Gupta has a Ph.D. in social psychology from Bangalore University in India and has over ten years' experience in the fields of women's health and women in development. She is the author of several articles on gender and reproductive health and has helped to develop curriculum on women's health for a graduate programme at the Tata Institute of Social Sciences in Bombay, India.

Chee Heng Leng lectures in the Department of Nutrition and Community Health at the Universiti Pertanian Malaysia and has done research on the health care system in Malaysia. She is a member of the team currently carrying out a survey of the nutritional status of major occupational groups in Malaysia, as well as being a country representative member of the International Productive Rights Research and Action Group. She is a founder member of the All Women's Action Society, and the Women's Development Collective, in Malaysia.

Gudrun Lachenmann is Professor of Sociology at the Sociology of Development Research Centre of the Faculty of Sociology, University of Bielefeld. She specialises in women's issues in developing countries. She studied sociology, political science and economics at the University of Konstanz, and for several years was a researcher at the German Development Institute in Berlin. Her fields of interest now include transformation processes in developing countries, such as liberation, democratisation and changing development paradigms, and social security with a focus on social movements and gender. Her research in the field has been mainly in West Africa.

Cecilia Ng Choon Sim is a Lecturer at the Center for Extension and Continuing Education, Universiti Pertanian Malaysia. She has re-searched and published on issues pertaining to gender and technology in both rural and urban settings. At present, she is involved in a study on the impact of new technologies on women's industrial work in the Asia Pacific region at the United Nations University (Institute of New Technologies, Maastricht, The Netherlands).

Ruth Pearson is Senior Lecturer in Economics at the School of Development Studies, University of East Anglia. She has researched and published widely on issues of industrialisation and gender relations, women's movements and femisnism internationally, and reproductive health and rights. Her article, with Diane Elson 'The Subordination of Women and the Internationalization of Factory Production' in *Of Marriage and the Market* (1981, eds. Young K et al.) has deeply influenced debates on the subject. Geographically, her interests are in Latin America and the Carribbean, though she has also worked in the European context.

Ines Smyth has recently joined OXFAM, as a Policy Adviser, Gender, after teaching and researching in various academic institutes, most recently at the London School of Economics, where she continues to be an affiliate of the Gender Institute. She is interested in reproductive rights, gender and social policies, and rural industrialisation. Recent publications include a co-edited volume (with M. Grijns) *Different Women, Different Work: Gender and Industrialization in Indonesia* (1994, Aldershot: Avebury).

Gemma Tang Nain is Project Coordinator of the Caribbean Associa-tion for Feminist Research and Action, which was the NGO Focal Point for the Caribbean for the 1995 UN Conference on Women, Beijing. Her interests lie in gender policy and organisational devel-opment, focusing particularly on the gender effects in state social policies. Her recent publications include 'Black Women, Sexism and Racism' in S. Jackson (1993), *Women's Studies: A Reader,* Hemel Hempstead: Harvester Wheatsheaf.

ACKNOWLEDGEMENTS

This book is an outcome of the International Workshop on 'Insecurity in the 1990s: Gender and Social Policies in an International Perspective'. Thus, our first thanks go to all those who took part in the workshop. In particular, we wish to thank the authors of the presentations on which the chapters are based for coming together to share their considerable insights and experience, and for their perseverance during the long process of preparing this publication.

The workshop was supported financially by the Commission of the European Community (Unit V.B.4), and by the Fund for University Development Cooperation (FUOS) of the University of Amsterdam, and in other ways by the European Association of Development Institutes (EADI). To all institutions we wish to express our gratitude for making it possible to realise a project of this nature. Similarly, we are thankful to the London School of Economics where the workshop took place, and to its administrative staff and the students who lent enthusiastic hands. Rita Crowley-Turner undertook the task of copy-editing the original collection, and did so with patience and good humour. The publishers of the book have been supportive in all stages of the work, and of this we are very appreciative.

Finally, our immediate friends and families are to be, yet again, deeply thanked for creating the conditions which make work of this type less stressful and more enjoyable than would otherwise be possible.

1

SEARCHING FOR SECURITY

Women's Responses to Economic Transformations

Isa Baud and Ines Smyth

INSECURITY IN THE 1990s

The lives of billions of people are not merely nasty, brutish and short, they are also full of uncertain horrors. An epidemic can wipe out a community, a famine can decimate a nation, unemployment can plunge masses into extreme deprivation, and insecurity in general plagues a large part of mankind with savage persistence.

(Dreze and Sen, 1991: 3)

All human life has always entailed, by definition, a great deal of insecurity. But in developing countries precariousness and uncertainty are superimposed onto deprivation (Burgess and Stern, 1991), so that the combination of the two gives rise to conditions which not only make daily life less than satisfactory, but which profoundly affect the long-term and life prospects of individuals and their communities, and those of future generations.

This general insecurity has been increasing in recent years, for a number of reasons. One reason is the global economic crisis which, in the last two decades, has slowed down and even reversed many of the social and economic gains which developing countries had achieved in the 1960s and up to the early 1970s. Even more tragically, this negative trend has been aggravated by the very measures introduced to stabilise and adjust national economies all over the world. After a decade of criticism and alarms sounded at the negative impacts of structural adjustment programmes on the social sector, the short-comings of the reforms are now recognised even by their initiators and supporters (World Bank, 1989). Adjustment measures have in many cases deeply affected people's ability to earn their livelihood as a means of achieving security through productive work, and their access to the welfare provisions which should increase short- and long-term social and personal security. The latter problem has been particularly acute for the most vulnerable groups in society: the very poor, women and children (Cornia et al., 1987; Sparr, 1994).

A second major reason for the increasing insecurity is that familiar patterns of global political relations, alliances and rankings have been destroyed by momentous political transformations, which have led to very fluid international and regional situations in the 1990s. A particularly acute manifestation of this situation is the intensification of violence in regions of unresolved conflicts, and the emergence of new foci of armed struggles. In parts of the former Yugoslavia and Soviet Union, as well as in sections of the Middle East, in Angola, Sudan, East Timor and several other areas, insecurity now means living in life-threatening conditions. These developments come as an addition to the existing situation of economic vulnerability in which so many people in developing countries already live, and have thus increased the sources and manifestations of insecurity.

The third global threat to security is in the ecological sphere. Though there is acute disagreement on the origins and causes of such a threat, it is clear that the deterioration of the natural resources essential for human survival and well-being, and for those of other living species, is severe both at the local and global levels.

It is not only general living conditions which have become more insecure. In many cases, at the core of the problem is the fact that 'social security' institutions are experiencing crises and upheavals which seriously undermine their ability to perform their functions. Here we are not using the term 'social security' narrowly, as the programmes linked to welfare-state type provisions. Rather, we adopt the definition of Dreze and Sen, who see social security

> essentially as an objective pursued through public means rather than a narrowly defined set of particular strategies, and it is important to take a broad view of the broad means that are relevant to the attainment of this objective.
>
> (Dreze and Sen, 1989:16)

Through this broader perspective it is possible to see that people draw social security from many institutions: the household, the community, trade, religious and charitable organisations, the state. The upheavals and crises mentioned above create strong challenges to their ability to enhance the security of the individuals for whom they are responsible. These challenges and problems are many and diverse.

At the level of the more informal institutions, households and communities are the most directly affected by recent crises, since they represent the first line of defence against the consequences of a collapse in security. Institutions such as non-governmental organisations (NGOs), are often assigned tasks for which they are not always prepared and for which they have insufficient resources and capabilities.

The most dramatic challenges are faced by the state. The attack against the state comes from two opposite sources (Mackintosh, 1992). On the one hand, it comes from those who regard state institutions as inefficient, unresponsive to the needs of citizens and corrupt. From this perspective, the requirement to streamline state institutions and reduce expenditures has led to the privatisation of certain services, and to cost recovery measures, introduction of fees and targeting of interventions in others. The consequences for social welfare of the adoption of such measures have been amply documented (Cornia et al., 1987; Ghaih, 1991 and many others).

The attack on the state has also come from those who are preoccupied by the top-down, undemocratic nature of state programmes. They have tended to seek in the community – and especially in grassroots and non-governmental organisations – the agencies capable of taking on the responsibility of social policies (Thomas, 1992). As said earlier, such institutions are thus confronted with responsibilities which necessitate a fundamental reconsideration of their aims and organisation.

Looking at which agencies should or could take up the task of providing security has led also to considering how institutions emerge and how they work internally, how different state institutions relate to other types of civil institutions or organisations and with what results (IDS Bulletin, 1992; EADI, 1993).

GENDER PERSPECTIVE ON INSECURITY

To what extent does a gender perspective emerge from such discussions? The study of social welfare and social policies, as well as the practice, have traditionally had a problem with gender differences and inequalities. They have often ignored the specific and varied experiences of women. When women have been noticed, it has been as targets of welfare-oriented interventions (Buvinić, 1986). As many feminist scholars have observed, this reflects the fact that women are perceived as enclosed by the family or the household. Their main responsibilities are defined in terms of bearing and caring for children, and other dependent members of the household and the community. The result, in terms of the theory and practice of social policies, has been for women to be treated as eternal dependants, appendages of their fathers or husbands.

We have progressed a great deal from these positions. There is ample documentation that women are more than just carers or dependants (see Joekes, 1987, for an overview). There is also evidence that women in general and certain categories of women in particular occupy social positions which result in their being both most vulnerable to crises and most responsible for the security of others. The literature on the impact of structural adjustment on women is particularly plentiful (see Afshar and Dennis, 1992, for a useful bibliography). Also advanced are the analyses of the ways in which gender operates as one of the key variables in social and economic transformations (witness the debate on abortion laws in the German parliament during the reunification process), the gendered nature of social welfare institutions, such as state bureaucracies, trade unions or NGOs, and the relative ability of the different institutions to incorporate in their activities a responsiveness to women's perspectives which is effective and long lasting (Staudt, 1990; Goetz, 1992).

Two main questions related to the discussions above have been taken as the focus of the contributions to this volume. The first concerns the effects on women of the insecurity-inducing global changes outlined earlier. Although, as already noted, it is difficult to disentangle economic, environmental and political changes, the emphasis here is mainly on economic transformations and their impact. This impact was understood as either direct, through the implementation of new policies and of public sector reforms, and of (nationally or internationally sponsored) programmes in specific areas of social welfare and social policy, or as indirect, through the interplay of cross-sectoral changes in trends and strategies.

The second question addresses the issue of how women have reacted to such changes. Though inevitably the individual level is considered, the focus has been primarily on how women have developed institutional responses to such changes and threats, in search of security but also of the more ambitious and long-term goal of empowerment.

The contributions to the volume address these questions for different countries and regions, but also for different social sectors and, to some extent, different categories of women. As a consequence, they provide analyses and illustrations which cross several levels of comparison and reveal many contrasts and similarities. Given the diversity of the accounts and analyses provided by the contributors, it is clearly unrealistic to try to identify answers to the two questions posed that are final and universally applicable. But some general observations can be drawn from the contents of the chapters.

In relation to the first question, namely the impact on women of changes in specific social conditions and social policies, it is obvious that overall social conditions have increased women's insecurity, while social policies are increasingly less accessible and beneficial to women. However, this negative assessment is tempered by two considerations. One is the realisation that there are enormous variations in both aspects, across countries and sectors, as well as in the categories of women most directly affected. The other is the awareness that, because of the gendered nature of social policies and of the pervasiveness of gender norms, women in general, and the poorest ones in particular, have always adopted self-reliant strategies which have lessened their dependence on public policies.

The second question addresses the issue of how women have reacted to such changes in terms of developing institutional, rather than individual, responses. Various authors have stressed the importance of women's own organisations, and have done so at various levels: from the recognition of the resilience of such organisations and of the need for community-based social policy to maintain such initiatives in the face of armed conflicts and other extreme situations, to the reaffirmation of the importance of strengthening the role of autonomous, local organisations as alternatives to a retreating state. Writing on specific sectors, the authors have indicated the significance of women's organisations in:

1 setting independent agendas reflecting women's needs;
2 improving the accountability and responsiveness of state institutions to women as both citizens and members of bureaucracies;
3 reducing the use of women as instruments in the implementation of state policies and reforms;
4 lobbying to increase women's access to state bureaucracies and other development agencies.

The validity of these observations cannot be over-stressed, since they strike a balance between acknowledging the importance of the autonomy and creativity typical of women's organisations, and the need to realise the danger of entirely exonerating the state from fulfilling its social responsibilities towards women as citizens.

OVERVIEW OF THE CONTRIBUTIONS

In this volume, the separate chapters are grouped in two sets. The first set includes those chapters (Pearson, Tang Nain and Lachenmann) which address the two questions in general terms, focusing on the relation between state and civil society, and on the broad transformations and policy reorientations which have altered this relationship. The second set contains the chapters (Beall, Adamik, Chee and Ng, Buvinić and Rao Gupta) which deal with the two questions by documenting and analysing these issues from the perspective of specific sectors, namely health, social security, employment, and poverty-alleviation programmes for female-headed households.

Chapter 2 addresses the first of the two questions by outlining the extent to which the increase in armed conflicts has contributed to global insecurity for women and children. In particular, Pearson remarks on how existing social services, designed to support women's reproductive role, are being annihilated by conflict or put out of reach of women, and on the extent to which such conflicts undermine women's control over their own sexuality. For Pearson, such situations illustrate the changing role of the state, retreating from the role of central arbiter and setter of standards, to that of one among many actors. This implies that organisations attempting to make policies sensitive to gender-related issues need to adapt their strategies accordingly. Pearson singles out the policy areas of population growth and environmental degradation as examples of areas where women are perceived as central to the effective implementation of policies. She considers it essential to overcome the tendency of policymakers to use women as instruments of policies, rather than as equal actors in the process of policy determination.

Chapter 3 deals with the first of the two questions by tracing the development of state interventions in the English-speaking Caribbean and the relationship between social policies and women from the 1960s to the present day. The second question is answered by showing the increasing importance of NGOs in the region, as effective agents for making the state more 'accountable' to their citizens, particularly in the context of the structural adjustment programmes adopted in the region.

Chapter 4 discusses recent developments in Africa in relation to the disengagement of the state and the growth of the private sector and the market. In reply to the second question, Lachenmann suggests that although the destabilising process of structural adjustment may challenge autonomous social institutions, these still represent a crucial source of security for the majority of women. She recommends that such autonomous groups be supported by international agencies as an alternative to state-funded social security.

Chapter 5, the first with a sectoral focus, discusses the first question by documenting the changes in health policies and practices over the last three decades. Beall concentrates on the change from curative healthcare, vertically structured, toward primary healthcare delivered in a more horizontal fashion, and on the implicit ideas on gender relations within these approaches. The latter have led to a concentration of attention on maternal and childcare, to the exclusion of poor men and of women in other than their childbearing roles. The recent economic crises have meant increases in the cost of healthcare and have shifted the burden of care onto communities, with different effects on men and women. Targeting has led to women being drawn into programmes on a voluntary basis, and with little or no training being offered to them. As her contribution to the second question, Beall suggests that a viable alternative is to be found in the empowerment approach, which emphasizes women's self-reliance in combination with the 'Human Development' approach currently promoted by the international agencies, which can provide a standard for women's groups to evaluate future state initiatives.

Chapter 6 attempts to answer the two questions for the case of a society in transition, that of Hungary. Adamik describes the Hungarian state-led system of social benefits as almost exclusively composed of employment-related benefits (crèches for working mothers, sick leave and maternity leave). Since the demise of the regime in the late 1980s, the reaction against all things 'communist' has included reactions against women's employment and social security benefits, despite the fact that large sections of the population currently live on incomes below the poverty line. The newly established Social Security Fund, paid for by employers and employees and much more targeted than before, is only a very partial solution to the loss of existing benefits. Adamik suggests that fundamental changes in gender relations, and in the relations between the state and its citizens, are still to be made.

As their attempt at replying to the first question in Chapter 7, Chee and Ng examine the impact of Malaysia's economic policies on women workers, focusing particularly on the impact of industrial restructuring. Although Malaysia did not suffer the heavy penalties of structural adjustment prevalent elsewhere, the impact has been on the quality of employment and on the bargaining power of workers. There has been an increase in subcontracting relations and casualisation of employment, as well as an increase in flexibilisation and job intensification. This situation has stifled the rights of women workers despite their participation in labour organisations and related struggles.

Finally, Chapter 8 considers the impact on women of one specific type of social policy. Buvinić and Rao Gupta examine the case of female-headed households, which in the majority of developing countries are not reached by state social policies. Targeting the poorest and most vulnerable groups in society has been mooted recently as a method of decreasing the costs of social policy while simultaneously improving its effectiveness. They look at the cases of Chile and India, where such households have been specifically targeted in state-led social programmes, to see what the positive and negative effects of doing so are for the women concerned. According to the authors, the two country experiences show that targeting female-headed households can represent an effective component of anti-poverty policies. At the same time they demonstrate the need for caution in the design and implementation of these programmes, to avoid unacceptably high costs, leakages and political backlashes which would ultimately damage the women and the households such programmes are intended to support.

REFERENCES

Afshar, H. and Dennis, C. (eds) (1992) *Women and Adjustment Policies in the Third World*, London: Macmillan.

Burgess, R. and Stern, N. (1991) 'Social Security in Developing Countries: What, Why, Who and How?' in E. Ahmad, J. Dreze, J. Hill and A. Sen (eds) *Social Security in Developing Countries*, Oxford: Clarendon Press.

Buvinić, M. (1986) 'Projects for Women in the Third World: Explaining their Misbehaviour' in *World Development* 14, 5: 653–664.

Cornia, G., Jolly, R. and Stewart, F. (eds) (1987) *Adjustment with a Human Face*, Oxford: Oxford University Press.

Dreze, J. and Sen, A.K. (1989) *Hunger and Public Action*, Oxford: Clarendon Press.

Dreze, J. and Sen, A.K.(1991) 'Public Action for Social Security: Foundation and Strategy' in E. Ahmad, J. Dreze, J. Hill and A. Sen (eds) *Social Security in Developing Countries*, Oxford: Clarendon Press.

EADI (European Association of Development Institutes) (1993) Proceedings of the General Conference 1993, Berlin.

Ghai, D. (1991) *The IMF and the South: The Social Impact of Crisis and Adjustment*, London: Zed Books.

Goetz, A. M. (1992) 'Gender and Administration' in *IDS Bulletin* 23,4: 1–15.

IDS Bulletin (1992) 'New Forms of Public Administration' 23, 4.

Joekes, S. (1987) *Women in the World Economy: An INSTRAW Study*, Oxford: Oxford University Press.

Mackintosh, M. (1992) 'Questioning the State' in M. Wutys, M. Mackintosh and T. Hewitt, *Development Policy and Public Action*, Oxford: Oxford University Press.

Sparr, P. (ed.) (1994) *Mortgaging Women's Lives: Feminist Critiques of Structural Adjustment*, London and New Jersey: Zed Books.

Staudt, K. (ed.) (1990) *Women, International Development and Politics: The Bureaucratic Mire*, Philadelphia: Temple University Press.

Thomas, S. (1992) 'Non-governmental Organisations and the Limits to Empowerment' in M. Wutys, M. Mackintosh, and T. Hewitt, *Development Policy and Public Action*, Oxford: Oxford University Press.

World Bank (1989) *Sub-Saharan Africa: From Crisis to Sustainable Growth*, Washington, DC: World Bank.

2

GLOBAL CHANGE AND INSECURITY

Are Women the Problem or the Solution?

Ruth Pearson

INTRODUCTION

Tackling the subject of women and global change in the context of international insecurity in the 1990s illustrates an important recent change in ideas; a shift from considering women and gender relations within the framework of development to considering these issues in a truly international way – North and South, East and West, in which the context is not one of 'development' (see, for example, Grant and Newland, 1991; or Rowbotham and Mitter, 1994). This is a serious shift, as most researchers in this area have for a long period been working within a gender and development framework; i.e. examining the development process through a gender lens, and assessing development from a gender perspective.

Why is this shift important? First, because increasingly, the agenda of development is becoming more and more restrictive. Development increasingly means the set of economic and social policies, often, though not always, dreamed up outside countries where they are applied by a set of international experts – which are intended to affect the *material condition* of people, both men and women. Development means intervention by a development agency – a state, an international organisation, an NGO, in the lives of (poor) people with the laudatory aim of improving their situation – of meeting their basic needs.

Although this endeavour – of improving the lives and prospects of people for whom development policy is designed – is laudable, the ways in which 'gender policies' have been integrated increasingly leave one feeling as if such policies exist almost purely on paper. The international organisations, the research and teaching organisations, the well-meaning NGOs have put 'women on the agenda'; bilateral

10

and multilateral agencies are insisting that their staff have gender awareness training; technical assistance projects are monitored for their gender impact; there are women – even some feminists – who have achieved important positions in the hierarchy of these organisations. Nevertheless, the feeling remains that in spite of what they say, gender policies are not making sense, nor any difference in the usual activities of these organisations (IDS Bulletin, 1995).

Increasingly, one is left with the feeling that the important contexts and issues which affect women's lives lie outside of this 'development' world, in the *realpolitik* of international relations on the one hand, and in the policymaking international fora on the other, which while determining the direction and magnitude of international financial flows, cannot really be called development organisations. Both set parameters and constraints on macroeconomic and social policy in developing and other countries. In these contexts, together with the private lives of households, families and communities where gender relations and identities are constructed, women are seen as the problem at the heart of poverty, underdevelopment, environmental degradation, population growth, or – or even simultaneously – as the solution.

In this chapter, some of the major issues relating to gender and social policy in an international perspective are outlined, and an analytical framework is suggested which might help to forge policies in the 1990s and beyond.

GLOBAL INSECURITY AND COMMUNITY SOCIAL POLICY

First, the problem of global insecurity itself needs to be considered. The end of the cold war has not meant a cessation in international or intranational armed and military conflict; on the contrary, the world is witnessing an escalation in the number of armed confrontations – both high- and low-intensity conflicts – in the Gulf, Kurdhistan, Central America, Somalia, Bosnia, Palestine, Tajekistan, Mozambique, Angola, India, Sri Lanka, Peru and Rwanda/Burundi. These conflicts cover a wide range of political situations. Some of them are still echoes of the conflicts between the ex-superpowers seeking a political regime which reflects their ideological or strategic interests; others represent struggles for hegemony within national states, or struggles to destroy the patterns of former national states and replace them with new political entities. Still others represent struggles to assert or replace regional, ethnic or religious domination within old or new state structures.

The end of the old world order has ushered in a new world disorder, in which insecurity rather than security, armed conflict rather than 'democratic' or other political forms are the principal means of articulating conflicting interests. While one has been conditioned to think of war and armed conflict in the twentieth century as being exceptional, the possibility has to be faced that it may be becoming the norm, the actual reality for increasing portions of the world's population (Tickner, 1992).

Armed conflict and military action are not the only ways in which global insecurity is changing the parameters of the world order. In many situations where there is not (as yet) overt military conflict, the old structures of the state are disappearing, or have disappeared, or are in the process of extreme modification. The most obvious example is the former Soviet Union, the least obvious is the curtailment of local government in the United Kingdom. The role of the supernational organisations within the United Nations system is also changing. It is increasingly required to play a belligerent – if policing – role within inter- and intranational conflicts, with its development activities marginalised in favour of operational activities and emergency actions.

What are the implications of the recognition that armed conflicts and the emergency state are becoming the norm rather than the exception? One of the most direct ways in which this affects women is how they carry out biological reproductive activities – conceiving and having babies. Normally, when we talk of reproduction, we generally refer to forms of social reproduction: nurturing infants and children, reconstituting male and female labour power on a daily as well as a generational basis, looking after those who are unable to use their labour power to secure (part) of their own reproduction costs – the sick, the infirm and the elderly (Sen, 1994). The conditions for carrying out these activities are constantly inadequate, and the assumptions about the financial resources made available for these activities are one of the major problems of male-biased economic and social policies in many countries.

However, the focus here is on other elements of women's reproductive role – sexuality and childbirth – which ironically have often been absent from feminist analyses of development, or from international relations.[1] A Ugandan woman told me the following story, in the context of a conversation about the reproductive responsibilities of women compared to men. She told of a friend and colleague who was pregnant during the civil war in Uganda in the early 1980s. The woman had a breach baby. But at the point at which she went into labour, there was a curfew and as a result the baby was born with no medical attention, causing great suffering and damage to the mother, and causing irreversible and considerable brain damage to the baby, who requires constant physical care. The woman later had a second, healthy child. The husband tried to subject the disabled daughter to traditional healers, which the mother considered harmful and which she opposed. As a result, the husband deserted her, took the healthy child with him, and provides no material support for the mother or the child left with her.

Armed conflict can thus destroy all the material advances of social policies and investment which are designed to offer appropriate services for women fulfilling their reproductive role in childbirth. As is known, in the former Yugoslavia even a relatively sophisticated infrastructure of health and other services can be annihilated by conflict. But services do not have to be destroyed by armed conflict – they just have to be removed from the reach of women needing them by military blockades, by curfews, by destruction of communications or transport, by the interruption of the whole social fabric on which they depend.

In analysing social policies we should therefore take into account two aspects which this example illustrates; first, that regardless of the rhetoric about the priority of social policies to support women's reproductive role, these services will be suspended because of military and political conflict, which is becoming a more common reality in global terms. However, women's reproductive activities cannot be suspended. Therefore, policies and services which are *sustainable* within communities need to be considered, rather than relying on the provision of centralised services which, despite their efficiency in conventional economic terms, cannot be guaranteed during emergencies.

A second aspect related to the implications of global insecurity is the issue of *sexuality*. Even in times which we have learned to think of as normal, women's control over their sexuality – including the circumstances and the conditions under which they allow or enjoy sexual activity – is severely constrained by patriarchal gender relations. In a war or conflict situation even socially accepted patterns are destroyed as rape becomes a mechanism in which women's sexuality is used instrumentally to further strategic or political ends.

13

In Europe we cannot ignore the fact that the rape of women across social and age ranges has been used as a deliberate policy by Serbs (and perhaps by other groups) in an attempt to dominate and/or eliminate the viability and claims of minority populations. Systematic use of rape as part of military action is an acknowledged feature of military conflict in many contexts; it was used in military action in Uganda in the 1980s, and in the war in East Bengal in 1968 which resulted in the establishment of the State of Bangladesh; we know that rape was used against minority groups in Kuwait during the Gulf war; we know that both sides raped women in occupied and liberated parts of the war theatre during and after the Second World War.

Rape and other forms of sexual humiliation and torture have been a commonplace practice during the 'dirty wars' against the left wing 'enemy within' in Argentina and the left in Chile in the 1970s; Amnesty International has documented the use of rape and sexual torture against political prisoners by government security forces in many countries in the world (Amnesty International, 1995). It is probably only the fact that the electronic media have given the rest of the world contemporaneous knowledge of the ongoing situation in the former Yugoslavia which has made it a matter of discussion at international fora such as the EU and the UN; most of the widespread abuses by armed forces only come to the attention of the rest of the world some time after they are committed. Using physical power to appropriate women's capacity for sexuality and biological reproduction is currently manifested when the rape of Bosnian Muslims is justified in terms of forcing them to reproduce Serbian babies rather than Muslims.

However, the *alienation* of women's sexual and biological capacity is best illustrated by a statement of the Pope that women who become pregnant as the result of rape in Bosnia should not terminate these pregnancies, but accept and nurture the child. What can 'safe motherhood' mean when it is clear that it does not include any notion that women themselves should have some say over the conditions in which they exercise their reproductive capacities? If the objectives of safe motherhood are defined in terms of the priorities of the community, nation or collectivity, or even of 'development', not even a beginning has been made to formulate a social policy which affords women any kind of agency or subjectivity in carrying out their reproductive activities.

A third implication of global insecurity concerns the modification and in some cases the withdrawal of the state itself from social policies.

This is most clear in situations of drastic political change and conflict. Many of the social policies which have tried to ensure that women are taken into account and are gender sensitive, assume the existence of a state which has powers of resource allocation, powers of political and social support for 'liberal' equality and judicial fairness, has powers to initiate proactive and prefigurative action to protect women and to direct social change in the interests of women and gender equity. Examples include campaigns against dowry murder, domestic violence, and innovative policies to provide credit to women micro-entrepreneurs, to provide housing and income generation opportunities for female-headed households, and to increase educational opportunities for girls.

Increasingly, however, such social policies and campaigns will be conducted in situations where the state has changed, has died or has transformed itself into something else. The enabling and supporting state which offers some kind of juridical backdrop for social policy is being replaced by a state which regulates to preserve the opportunities for individual entrepreneurs and private organisations (including NGOs) against the encroachment of a powerful and counteracting state. Instead of a national campaign aimed at the Ministry of Health and Social Welfare which otherwise would provide the bench mark for gender-aware health and social security policy, the current reality is more likely to be a campaign aimed at a range of individual providers and private organisations, including NGOs (many of which are more effective and women-friendly than parallel state structures).

The point is that the state is no longer a central arbiter of standards and policies which have some universal applicability. This situation will drastically alter the ways in which policies which are designed to redress gender inequalities can be promoted.

THE INSTRUMENTAL USE OF WOMEN

A second feature of global change and insecurity is reflected by the macro-level policy environments of the 1990s in which women are incorporated into policy agendas, using women as instrumental solutions to 'development' or 'social' problems rather than assigning any subjectivity to women themselves.

There are two interconnecting fields in which such issues are relevant, which are discussed here; population growth and environmental degradation. In both these areas, it is clear that the recognition that women are central to the issue and therefore are to be influenced by policy in order to achieve solutions, is not premised on any understanding of women's agency in biological and social reproduction nor in the reproduction of the environment. Women are viewed instrumentally as part of the problem and thus of the solution.

Population growth

Because major policy institutions are concerned about the rate of population increase and the (often erroneous) association of over-population with underdevelopment, the introduction of family planning policies has been part of the conditionality of structural adjustment programmes introduced by the World Bank. Very often these are couched in terms of the necessity to promote maternal and child health, though in some cases it is clear that this is not the major objective of such policies. In Bolivia the Bank carried out a study in 1987 in which it maintained that an important obstacle to reducing population growth and high levels of fertility was the limited diffusion of contraceptives in the country. The document stated:

> The reduction of fertility has high priority for humanitarian, equity and economic reasons. The maternal and infant mortality and morbidity is strictly related to frequent births, poorly spaced, and is concentrated in poor families. The high rates of population growth exert strong pressures on the still insufficient capacity of employment creation and public sector services and impede the growth in per capita income. It is therefore a crucial necessity to satisfy the increasing demand for contraceptives for families who wish to use them but are not doing so. This can be achieved via horizontal and vertical programmes and integrated programmes of subsidised sales (to increase the supply of contraceptives via the pharmacies) and increasing female literacy.
>
> (Cited in Rance, 1990: 19–20)[2]

So the policy framework which is concerned about high population growth wishes to increase access to contraception in order to reduce the fertility rate – and the infant and maternal mortality rate of 'poor families' – which are an impediment to economic growth. Female literacy is a goal only to the extent that demographers and others widely believe that reduction in fertility is strongly correlated with increases in female literacy.[3]

16

Such policy windfalls for women are at best conditional and at worst misguided, given that the conditions under which family planning services are made available can range from the coercive to the supportive. The conditionality arises from the fact that such programmes do not increase women's ability to determine the conditions and circumstances under which they exercise their sexuality and their biological reproductive activities.

It is unclear at this moment what will happen to the considerable developments of family planning programmes in Bolivia, now that the interim results of the population census indicate that the rate of population growth is considerably lower than the estimates on which the World Bank's policy is formulated (Pearson and Durrant, 1992). In many other countries, governments have adopted pro-natalist policies to support a national priority of *population growth* rather than reduction, where incentives to reproduce are targeted at educated women, rather than the poor and illiterate.

The assumption that two policy targets can be reached with a single policy instrument – what the World Bank has called 'win-win' policies – are deeply flawed from the point of view of gender equity, however. Using women's literacy and education as a leverage to affect levels of fertility rather than underwriting any commitment to support redistribution of resources to women's education and health-care is a cynical reflection of the instrumentality of international development agencies' commitment to putting women on the development agenda.

Such policies disregard the actual conditions under which women exercise their sexuality and reproductive functions: gender relations in which women using contraception are equated with promiscuity, constructions of masculinity which are linked to high levels of marital fertility, and a political context which historically has not distinguished between coercive population control and family planning as a reproductive right.

Environmental degradation

The second area of global change and insecurity to be discussed here concerns environmental degradation. Again, it has been common to link the policy implications of macro issues – poverty alleviation, environmental conservation and women and development in what the United Kingdom's Overseas Development Administration (ODA) has termed 'synergistic interventions':

[The] identification of *synergistic interventions* which will act simultaneously on population–environment–poverty problems presents an obvious way forward. Improving the rights and livelihoods of women, or the wider notion of Primary Environmental Care, may be promising approaches.

(ODA, 1991, original emphasis, cited in Jackson, 1992: 18)

The problems with this approach are two-fold. First of all, it presents policies to support women's income earning opportunities solely in the context of their instrumentality in wider (more important) goals such as 'population–environment–poverty'. This is a potentially dangerous strategy, since it assumes there are no contradictions in this approach and that what is good for the environment will be good for women and vice versa.

However, if one considers the *reality* of the ways in which gender relations impinge on the practices and processes of livelihood systems which affect the environment, it is clear that there is not necessarily an automatic identity between women's interests and the interests of environmental conservation. The ways in which women relate to the land and natural resources are mediated through both class and gender identities. The relationship also changes with age and stages in the life-cycle, so that a uniform category of women as the instrumental access to environmental conservation is misplaced. Existing patterns of kinship and land tenure in fact will often mean that women's relationship with the land is temporary and mediated through marriage, so that they do not have any notion of long-term benefits from investing in conservation.

An example from Zimbabwe shows that where women work land only in the context of virilocal marriage, commitment to land improvement practices, such as building contour ridges and planting trees, are not rational for women. They are unlikely individually – or through their children – to reap any long-term benefit from them (Jackson, 1992: 29–30). Even where women depend on tree products for fuel wood for cooking, they may have no role in tree planting because of the nature of gender relations. Moreover, the necessity for women to obtain cash incomes leads many to undertake domestic beer-brewing, which requires the slow burning of fresh green wood rather than the dry dead foliage and wood used in domestic cooking.

There is no single relationship between women and nature, and attempts by policymakers to assume one are done at the expense of examining the complex reality of gendered activities which should be the guide to appropriate and gender-sensitive social policy.

CONCLUSIONS

What conclusions can one draw from this analysis? Aspects of global change and insecurity which in my view are central to the analysis of gender and social policy in the 1990s and which can be useful as a background for the following chapters are as follows. Social and economic policy must be informed by a comprehensive and contextualised understanding of the varied and conflicting nature of gender relations in different situations, rather than relying on some universal and timeless whole into which policies about women can be rhetorically dropped.

In spite of the increase of gender terminology in official rhetoric, it is not clear at the level of the macro policy environment that much progress has been made in this direction. The inclusion of the realities of women's reproductive activities against a backdrop of increasing global conflict and change in the 1990s, serves to illustrate the gap between the rhetoric and the reality.

We are confronted with the *presence* of women in the discourse. But their presence is not premised on an analysis or understanding of the nature of their *reproductive work* – just assumptions about their *reproductive role*. Moreover, the abstraction of reproduction to an idealised rather than a concrete understanding of what it involves and how it gets done, means that much social policy is formulated on assumptions about *ideal models* of social relations and social institutions, rather than confronting the range of actually existing relations and institutions.

This trend can be identified throughout the debates and analyses of a range of policies – housing, income support, credit provision, family planning, childcare and transport. They invariably assume a two-adult, male-headed nuclear family, a non-working/income- generating woman, with dependent children where decisions are made 'in the interests of all household members' and resources are shared according to priority of need.

Policies designed to meet the needs of other groups – female-headed households, single mothers, divorced women, survivors of domestic violence, refugees, teenage women seeking abortions, homeless adolescents on the streets of London – are always made on the assumption that these groups are minority deviants from the dominant ideal pattern, which reflects actual as well as desired reality. Special policies can be made on a residual targeted basis for the minority groups.

It is time that we insist that social policies be formulated with a much more realistic view of the *range* of patterns of social relations and institutions, so that they are *a priori* adaptable to different groups and situations. The dangers of not doing so can be illustrated in an example concerning policies to confront the pandemic of HIV (Human Immuno-deficiency Virus) and Aids (Acquired Immuno-deficiency Syndrome). In low-income countries[4] where there has been a high rate of infection with the HIV virus, it is very common for preventive policies to assume that the normal form of relationship which involves sexual relations is monogamous marriage. A more honest research enquiry in fact shows a range of relationships involving sexual exchange in not only marriage, but also formalised lover status, patron–client, commercialised transactions, temporary unions – as well as other more coercive relationships. However, policy discourse not only makes an assumption about monogamy, but also assumes that it is women who do not conform to this norm – i.e. 'prostitutes' – who are responsible for the transmission of the virus.

Given the reality of gender relations, in many cases this can result in a situation where wives of men who have other partners are at risk from infection, because of socially enforced assumptions about the pattern of sexual relations of their partners. At the same time women are unable to seek protection from infection, since they are denied control over the exercise of their own fertility by the use of contraceptives which could protect them, because there is a prevailing view that women who use such methods will be promiscuous. There is a wide range of relationships and unions in which sexual activity plays a part.[5] However, as long as this reality is ignored, the possibility of effective policies to prevent the spread of HIV/Aids will be small; and while women are particularly vulnerable because of their relative powerlessness over their sexuality and reproduction, they are also increasingly called on to assume the consequences of the high rates of mortality and morbidity – in terms of caring for the sick, for orphaned children and in substituting for agricultural and income-earning labour of affected male family members (Barnett and Blaikie, 1992).

Social and economic policy cannot just use women instrumentally in order to pursue other objectives and priorities. Such an approach may lead to policy stalemates because the failure to analyse gender relations seriously means that policy objectives are actually conflicting rather than complementary.

If changes in the policy context of the 1990s – including the recognition of continuing global conflicts, the transformed role of the state, the necessity for sustainable social and economic systems on a local as well as a global level – are to offer the possibility of transforming 'women and social policy' initiatives into initiatives that are honestly targeted at eliminating gender inequalities, then the reality of the range and complexity of gender relations needs to be recognised. This includes a realistic assessment of women's reproductive as well as productive work and the social relations which underlie them.

NOTES

1 Ironically, childbirth and sexuality have been absent from the discussions of women's reproductive work because, generally, discussion of the latter has been aimed to show the 'work-like' nature of such activity, its complementarity to productive work and therefore the necessity to include it in the macro and sectoral policy agenda. Also, feminists who have tried to utilise a materialist analysis of social relationships, including gender, have been careful to distance themselves from anything which might be dismissed as biological determinism and essentialism (see Sayers, 1982). As this debate has translated itself into development discourse, concern for improved maternal health, women's education and services to support women's nurturing role, and even to provide appropriate family planning services has not problematised women's relations with their sexual capacity or biological reproduction as a process or activity *in itself*. The fact that women are not only alienated from the products of their own reproductive activities – their children, and even their own labour – has been usefully discussed by Elson (1992). But this framework needs to be extended to problematise the autonomy women have over the conditions under which they have sexual intercourse, conceive and give birth, which is affected not just by interpersonal intrafamilial relations with male partners and other kin, but also by social norms, including socially legitimated or dissident religious beliefs and practices, the degree of autonomy they have to access information about reproductive health and practices, macro and sectoral economic and social policies which dictate the priority and absolute expenditure on health and other relevant services, *and* issues of international (in)security and military strategy which can override all of the above.
2 The fact that the political debate about family planning in Bolivia forced the Bank to modify this document – although not to modify its

policy of promoting family planning primarily in order to achieve economic growth – is discussed at length in Rance (1990) and Pearson and Durrant (1992).

3 Whether there is a direct correlation between female literacy or whether there is a dummy effect related to distribution and access to health and other services is disputed. See Bicego and Ties Boerma (1991).

4 My knowledge is based mainly on Ethiopia, Zambia and Uganda.

5 See Kemp (1993), which uses a livelihood framework to investigate the part which sexual activity plays in a range of exchange and affective relationships.

REFERENCES

Amnesty International (1995) *Human Rights are Women's Rights*, London: Amnesty International Publications.

Barnett, A. and Blaikie, P. (1992) *Aids in Africa*, London: Belhaven Press.

Bicego, G. and Ties Boerma, J. (1991) 'Maternal Education, Use of Health Services and Child Survival: An Analysis of Data from the Bolivia DHS Survey', DHS Working Papers, Institute for Resource Development Inc., Columbia, Maryland, USA.

Elson, D. (1992) 'Poverty and Development: A Gender Aware Analysis'. Paper prepared for the Seminar on 'Women In Extreme Poverty: Integration of Women's Concerns in National Development Planning', Division for Advancement of Women, United Nations Office, Vienna.

Grant, R. and Newland, K. (eds) (1991) *Gender and International Relations*, Milton Keynes: Open University Press.

IDS Bulletin (1995) 'Getting Institutions Right For Women in Development' 26, 3.

Jackson, C. (1992) 'Gender, Women and Environment: Harmony or Discord?' Gender Analysis In Development, Discussion Paper 6, School of Development Studies, University of East Anglia, Norwich.

Kemp, J. (1993) 'Sexual Exchange and Livelihood Strategies: Towards a Framework for Analysing the Risks of HIV Infection for Women in West Africa', Gender Analysis in Development, Discussion Paper 7, School of Development Studies, University of East Anglia, Norwich.

Pearson, R. and Durrant, K. (1992) 'Women's Education, Health and Feasibility Mission for Bolivia'. Report for Marie Stopes Consultancy, School of Development Studies, University of East Anglia, Norwich.

Rance, S. (1990) 'Planificacion Familiar: Se Abre el Debate', Secretaria Tecnica del Consejo Nacional de Poblacion, CONAPU, La Paz.

Rowbotham, S. and Mitter, S. (eds) (1994) *Dignity and Daily Bread: New Forms of Economic Organizing Among Poor Women in the Third World and First*, London: Routledge.

Sayers, J. (1982) *Biological Politics: Feminist and Anti-Feminist Perspectives*, London: Tavistock.

Sen, G. (1994) 'Reproduction: The Feminist Challenge to Social Policy' in G. Sen and R. Snow (eds) *Power and Decision: The Social Control of*

Reproduction, Harvard Series on Population and International Health, Harvard Centre for Population and Development Studies, Department of Population and International Health, Harvard School of Public Health, Boston, Mass.

Tickner, J. A. (1992) *Gender in International Relations: Feminist Perspectives on Achieving Global Security*, New York: Columbia University Press.

3

THE RETREAT OF THE STATE IN THE ENGLISH-SPEAKING CARIBBEAN

The Impact on Women and their Responses

Gemma Tang Nain

INTRODUCTION

The retreat of the state has characterised developing and industrialised countries alike during the 1980s and into the 1990s. This retreat has had disastrous consequences for poor citizens (and especially poor women) throughout the world – popularly referred to as the Third World – where debt repayment and structural adjustment have been the dominant themes used in justification of the retreat. The English-speaking Caribbean[1], as part of the Third World, has not been spared this development, though some territories have been more affected than others. Indeed, it is precisely in those territories where the state had gone the furthest in terms of playing a dominant role that the retreat has been most stark, namely Jamaica, Guyana and Trinidad and Tobago. In order to contextualise the impact on women and their responses, this chapter traces the development of the state in the English-speaking Caribbean through a discussion of social policy and state expansion in the 1960s and 1970s and the process of retreat in the 1980s and 1990s. It then looks at the relationship between changing social policy and women, the main focus being on this relationship in the period of state retreat and structural adjustment.

SOCIAL POLICY AND THE STATE: THE 1960s AND 1970s

To understand the development of social policy in the English-speaking Caribbean during this period of political independence for most of these states, one has to refer to the dominant socioeconomic paradigm prevailing at that time. Standing (1991) refers to the dominant macroeconomic framework for the period as 'social keynesianism', the essence of which, he argues, is that macroeconomic monetary and fiscal policy is geared towards full employment. This framework supported a mixed economy in which public investment and public ownership of certain industries were seen as necessary. Indeed, public expenditure was seen as the facilitating mechanism for long-term growth and industrial development.

Walker (1984) provides a wide and comprehensive definition of social policy. He states that it is concerned not only with the distribution of income and wealth, but with the distribution of social welfare and social resources. 'Social welfare' he defines as consisting of individual health and well-being, and of collective solidarity, and cooperation. 'Social resources' according to him, include not only income, assets and property but also health, education and the environment. For Walker (ibid.: 39–40), then, social policy is 'the rationale underlying the development and reproduction of social institutions that determine the distribution of resources, status and power between different groups in society. [It] determines the creation, distribution and reproduction of social welfare (and dis-welfare)'. In short, social policy is about 'distributive justice'.

This discussion of social policy allows us to assess the understanding of it which informed emergent states in the English-speaking Caribbean in the 1960s and 1970s.

The 1950s are often identified as the starting point of a home-spun development strategy in this region (Henry, 1988), a strategy popularly referred to as 'Industrialisation by Invitation' based on a model advanced by Arthur Lewis. During this period, according to Brown (1981), the perception of limits to state power was still popular and even the utilities, 'long regarded as proper areas for government ownership, remained for the most part foreign owned' (ibid.: 3). The situation changed dramatically during the next two decades, however. The 1960s saw the expansion of the state bureaucracy through the growth of statutory boards and corporations as well as other regulatory bodies. In the 1970s, the change was even more evident, with clearly stated policies emerging in Guyana in the form of 'cooperative socialism', and in Jamaica with the advent of 'democratic socialism'. While Trinidad and Tobago did not adopt any official 'labels', its 1972 White Paper did outline a new role for the state, stressing, in particular, local ownership and/or control of previously foreign-owned enterprises. The main thrust of this new role of the state was public ownership and public investment in an environment, both national and international, characterised by changing notions about the appropriate role of governments. As Brown aptly states:

> Thus, where up to and even after constitutional independence, the state's activity could reasonably be limited to an administrative and regulatory role, by the 1970s there was evidence of a significant change in perspectives on the state's functions ... responsibility for economic development [was] understood to mean not simply regulation and direction of economic activity by indirect means. Specifically, that responsibility could also be expected to include direct state intervention to ensure adequate growth of the national product as well as its equitable social and economic distribution.
>
> (Brown, 1981: 3)

While this process of increased state activity was much more pronounced for the larger territories of Guyana, Jamaica and Trinidad and Tobago, as highlighted above, a similar process was also taking place, albeit to a lesser degree, in some of the smaller territories, notably Antigua and St Kitts. Grenada, under the People's Revolutionary Government between 1979 and 1983, also followed this general trend but with a much more overt ideological justification. A recent study of the operations of public enterprises in the Caribbean, undertaken by the Caribbean Centre for Administration and Development (CARICAD), pointed to three main ideologies as forming the basis for the establishment of state enterprises in the Caribbean. These were given as socialism, nationalism and pragmatism (*Trinidad Express*, 16 May 1990). In Trinidad and Tobago, the government's Draft Medium Term Macro Planning Framework (DMTMPF) 1989–1995 cited, *inter alia*, the following reasons for government's involvement in productive activity:

1 the desire to exercise greater control over the so-called commanding heights of the economy;
2 the objective of accelerating economic development by launching pioneering investment activity in areas where unfamiliarity with the technological requirements might otherwise serve to inhibit private sector investments, because of the perception of high risk;
3 the undertaking of rescue operations to save jobs in privately-owned enterprises which were on the verge of closure.

(DMTMPF, July 1988: 9–10)

26

One can suggest, then, that governments in the English-speaking Caribbean adopted a rather broad view of social policy, along the lines suggested by Walker (1984), in that they created institutions through which attempts were made to redistribute resources, status and power among different groups within these societies. In social-infrastructural terms, social policy of this nature meant free education (from primary to tertiary level); free health services; provision of subsidised public transportation; provision of low-cost housing, either with low interest rates for mortgages or low rental rates; food subsidies and control of basic food prices. As in the case of other Third World countries, the financing for a significant part of infrastructural development came from overseas borrowing – an action that would haunt these territories in the years ahead as interest rates doubled and trebled in some cases. One estimate indicates that real interest rates rose by 30 per cent in just two years, 1980–1982 (McAfee, 1991).

The fact that in the 1980s and 1990s the state has retreated from this policy is indicative, some would argue, of the contradictions inherent in the capitalist economic system. According to Moon (1988:27), some have described this type of social policy as 'a strategic response to the dislocations of capitalism, temporarily enabling a repressive and irrational form of society to stave off fundamental change by blunting the edge of social conflict'. Standing (1991) notes that recession in several of the world's major economies in the late 1970s and during the 1980s produced an onslaught on Keynesian methods, assumptions and values. Monetarism, which holds that market forces can and do solve all economic problems, became the dominant paradigm and out of it developed 'the supply-side perspective that crystallised in the orthodox stabilisation structural adjustment strategy that has been promoted zealously in both developing and industrialised countries in the 1980s' (ibid.: 12). As we shall see in the next section, this new paradigm impacted upon the English-speaking Caribbean as it did elsewhere.

THE RETREAT OF THE STATE:
THE 1980s AND 1990s

Throughout the English-speaking Caribbean the state has been in retreat during the 1980s, particularly since the mid-1980s and into the early 1990s. While this retreat has been propelled largely by the policy dictates of the International Monetary Fund (IMF) and the World Bank, one has to view it within the changed international political and economic environment as stated above. The debates about the limits to state power have come full circle and this time around the advocates of a limited role for the state are attacking with full force. The real tragedy for the English-speaking Caribbean and the rest of the Third World is that we have had no say in this paradigm shift.

Towards the end of the 1970s and during the 1980s therefore, structural adjustment programmes (SAPs) have been imposed on many Third World countries, including those in the English-speaking Caribbean. The main motive for these SAPs is to restructure economies so that enough foreign exchange can be earned to service accumulated debt. While these programmes vary to some degree from country to country, the main aims are to increase exports and hence earn foreign exchange, and to decrease domestic consumption. In the English-speaking Caribbean, for example, heads of government at a CARICOM summit in the Bahamas in the early 1980s called for 'measures to contract demand through drastic reductions in public and private consumption expenditure, the compression of imports and more restrictive monetary policies' (Massiah, 1985: 7). In terms of policy measures this has meant, *inter alia*, currency devaluations; reduction or removal of subsidies on basic goods and services; new forms of indirect and regressive taxation; cutbacks on government spending on social services; reduction of the workforce and wage cuts in the public services; and privatisation of state enterprises.

To illustrate the nature and extent of the retreat, the territories of Jamaica and Guyana will be used as examples. Reference will also be made to Trinidad and Tobago.

Jamaica

Jamaica's retreat started with its encounter with the IMF in 1977. As Levitt (1991) remarked, it signalled a turning point in the government's economic management of the country. She asserts that from that period, adjustment took priority over development, and the government was 'increasingly transformed into the local executing authority of programmes designed by the Washington-based agencies' (ibid.: 24). The full impact of SAPs was felt by the mid-1980s when massive devaluations, price and tax increases, discontinuation of food subsidies and extensive cuts in government expenditure resulted in a fundamental restructuring of the Jamaican economy. On the one hand, the IMF set the macroeconomic limits within which the government could function with respect to fiscal, credit and exchange rate policy, as well as wage guidelines. On the other hand, the World Bank directed and monitored the thrust towards economic liberalisation through the discontinuation of subsidies, full cost pricing of utilities and divestment of state enterprises, to highlight just some of the actions undertaken (Levitt, 1991).

The effect of these measures on the social infrastructure of Jamaica has been phenomenal. The health services, education, public transportation and low-cost housing have all become 'casualties' in the wake of structural adjustment 'assaults'. In the area of health, real per capita outlays declined from US$44 per capita in 1982–1983, to US$25.6 in 1986–1987, a reduction of 42 per cent. In terms of the percentage of public expenditures allocated to health, there was a steady decline from 10 per cent in 1969–1970 to 6 per cent in 1987–1988, as capital expenditure on health centres and hospitals virtually ceased (Levitt, 1991). The situation with respect to education is very similar, with per capita public expenditure declining from US$84 in 1981–1982 to US$58 in 1986–1987, a reduction of 32 per cent. The percentage of public expenditure allocations declined from 16 per cent in 1969–1970 to 11 per cent in 1987–1988, with schools suffering the same fate as health centres and hospitals with regard to capital expenditure (ibid.). This trend has of course impacted negatively on the quality of education provided and the outcome has been falling performance levels of Jamaican students. Further, as of 1986, a tax has been levied on all students acquiring tertiary education. Low-cost housing and public transportation have simply ceased to be considered the responsibility of government. Levitt (1991) has correctly described the situation as that of 'privatised' social services, given that the state-run services have deteriorated to such an extent that only the very poor and destitute continue to use them. Quality service is available, but at significant cost. Studies have revealed that 40 per cent of the very poorest quintile of the population now visit private doctors, at prices they realistically cannot afford, in order to receive better-quality medical care.

Another by-product of the diminished role of the state in Jamaica is a widening of the gap between rich and poor citizens. In the late 1980s, according to Levitt (1991), a chief executive officer in a large private sector company in Jamaica could have earned as much as J$1,000,000 per annum, while the minimum wage (for domestic workers) was J$4,368 per annum, a difference of 229 per cent. Similarly, increases in the salaries of top civil servants and members of parliament put their annual salaries in the vicinity of J$280,000 to J$370,000. While these salaries remained way below those paid for similar positions in the private sector, they were 64–85 per cent higher than the annual minimum wage and 15–20 per cent higher than the annual salary of a nurse or primary school teacher.[2] A system of food stamps has been introduced to assist the poor, the argument being that this is more effective in reaching only the poor, whereas the previous food subsidies benefited poor and rich alike, but such a system fails to take account of the issue of human dignity. Moon (1988: 32), in reference to pronouncements made by Raymond Plant, noted that for welfare not to be stigmatising it must be granted as a right rather than as a matter of charity. But, as noted by Levitt (1991: 41), within the changed value system of Jamaica in the 1980s, the 'poor' are 'really not considered to be people'.

Guyana

The retreat of the state in Guyana has been due, largely, to a virtual collapse of the Guyanese economy, but according to members of a fact-finding mission to Guyana in 1990, the structural adjustment programme (referred to as an Economic Recovery Programme by the Guyanese government of the period) is likely to exacerbate rather than solve the problem.[3] The report of the mission pointed to exogenous and endogenous factors leading to the collapse of the economy. The former are related to falling commodity prices and the rising price of imports, which served to increase Guyana's debt burden. The latter are linked to politicisation of almost every aspect of Guyanese existence and the mass exodus of most of the country's skilled personnel, leading to over-extended management and mis-management. Repercussions in the economy resulted in significant declines in the production of Guyana's main exports – sugar, rice and bauxite – during the late 1980s, resulting in diminished earnings. These factors have combined to produce, in the words of Levitt (1990), 'societal disintegration'.

The mission noted that the majority of Guyanese are no longer provided with the societal infrastructure necessary to meet their basic needs. Services such as education, healthcare, solid waste manage-ment, the supply of water, electricity and telephone services, have all suffered drastic deterioration. 'In the capital city of Georgetown, such basic services as garbage collection, the clearance of drains, and the provision of safe drinking water are no longer available' (Caribbean Conference of Churches (CCC), 1990: 24).

To compound the situation massive devaluations have rendered work in the formal sector useless, and so persons either combine work in the formal sector with work in the informal sector as traders or taxi drivers, or they abandon salaried work altogether. In 1985, the official exchange rate was G$4.15 to US$1.00. By early October 1990 it had jumped to G$45.00 to US$1.00, with the street rate at G$89.00 to US$1.00. Given this scenario,

> The absurdity of current wage levels is reflected by the fact that the remittance of US$20.00 from a relative abroad will provide a greater quantum of Guyanese dollars on the street than from a month of employment in many jobs in the formal sector, including many teaching positions.
>
> (ibid.: 11)[4]

The Guyanese therefore rely heavily on such remittances, as well as on the 'barrel' of foodstuffs and other basic items from abroad, which provides goods not only for individual and household consumption but also for sale on the streets.

Members of the same fact-finding mission were extremely critical of the structural adjustment programme which offered the standard recipe: privatisation, devaluation, the free reign of market forces. They argued that even if one ignored the flaws in the recipe, Guyana simply did not represent a typical case:

> Even within the 'laissez faire' economic philosophy, there is the concession that there are periods [sic] when abnormal economic conditions preclude the possibility of reliance merely on free market forces. . . . Under such conditions, even the most hardened free marketeer will concede the need for some prior stage of reconstruction of physical infrastructure and productive capacity, before market forces can be of effect.
>
> (ibid.)

The mission pointed to the examples of Europe after the Second World War and the more recent case of Eastern Europe. Therefore, according to the mission, what Guyana needs is a reconstruction programme along the lines of a mini-Marshall Plan.

Trinidad and Tobago

Like Jamaica, the retreat of the state in Trinidad and Tobago is a result of the implementation of SAPs, but this has occurred roughly ten years after the Jamaican experience. Trinidad and Tobago, with an oil-based economy, benefited from the booms of the 1970s and so was able to delay its encounter with SAPs until the late 1980s. The standard recipe has been applied and Trinidad and Tobago has had to cope with devaluation, privatisation, wage cuts in the public sector, cutbacks in government spending on social services and the introduction of several user charges with respect to health and tertiary education.

The ideological debate in Trinidad and Tobago concerning the appropriate role of the state has been an interesting one. Frank Rampersad, speaking at the Caribbean Studies Association Conference in Trinidad and Tobago in 1990, stated that while Caribbean governments needed to invest in economic ventures that are considered important and which are not being taken up by local private or foreign investors, it does not follow that they should retain control indefinitely. His advice was that having taken the initiative, the government should then pass the venture(s) on to the private sector (*Trinidad Express*, 25 May 1990). Gordon Draper, one of the consultants involved in the recent CARICAD Study mentioned earlier, holds a somewhat different view. He feels that state enterprises should definitely be retained, though issues of priority and management need to be addressed. He is of the opinion that in the Trinidad and Tobago context, the oil companies should definitely be retained by the state. The trade union movement has articulated a view similar to that of Draper.

While the gap in the standard of living between rich and poor citizens has definitely widened as a consequence of SAPs, within the public sector it has been somewhat restrained as a result of the militancy of the trade union movement. This movement has been fighting against retrenchment in the public sector (though it has occurred and is continuing) and, quite recently, it forced the government to rescind a decision to pay itself increased salaries while owing money to public servants.

From the foregoing it has been demonstrated that the dominance of the state in the 1960s and particularly the 1970s has been replaced by a hasty retreat in the 1980s and 1990s. The collapse of the socialist world and the communist ideology has served to strengthen the position of those advocating a limited role for the state, and it would seem that unbridled capitalism has become the order of the day. How, one might ask, have all these developments impacted on women in the English-speaking Caribbean? Has there been differential impact along gender lines? The next section will attempt to address these issues.

CHANGING SOCIAL POLICY: ITS IMPACT ON WOMEN, AND THEIR RESPONSES

This section will address two main periods: the era of political independence and state expansion, and the era of the retreat of the state. Before doing that, however, it is important to look briefly at the colonial era.

It is now well documented that with the abolition of slavery in the 1830s, the social policy pursued by the colonial authorities differed along gender lines. Not only were women paid less than men from the outset of wage labour, but a much more rigid sexual division of labour (SDL) was established and the domestic ideology of a male breadwinner and a dependent female housewife was actively promoted. By the 1930s a clearer policy could be discerned through the Education Code of 1935, which mandated the teaching of domestic science to girls only and prohibited the employment of married women as teachers. This was followed in 1939 by the Employment of Women (Night-Work) Ordinance, which prohibited women from working in industrial enterprises at night (Reddock, 1984).

Throughout this period, women did not remain passive. Women's self-help societies were formed in Jamaica, Trinidad and Tobago, and Barbados at the beginning of the twentieth century, to promote employment for women in spite of the dominance of the domestic ideology. Other important organisations included the Women's Social Service Club formed in Jamaica in 1918 and the Coterie of Social Workers founded by Audrey Jeffers in Trinidad and Tobago in 1921. Both organisations insisted on women enjoying full rights as human beings, not only in the home but in public activities as well. Women were also active in the disturbances of the 1930s and in the nationalist movements that emerged thereafter.

The era of political independence and state expansion: the 1960s and 1970s

Women, education and employment

The two areas of social policy which had a significant impact on women during this period were the expansion of education and the dominant role played by the state in economic activity. Free education, from primary school to tertiary level, provided women with a range of educational opportunities which they actively pursued. True sex-stereotyping remained in the various curricula but this was much less pronounced, except in the area of technical/vocational training where sex-stereotyping has remained entrenched. The expansion of the state sector into non-traditional areas opened up employment for all citizens, including women, and here, theoretically at least, women were offered an opportunity for entry and promotion based on the universal criteria of achievement (Tang Nain, 1992a). The point must be made, however, that throughout the period women remained insignificant in terms of official labour force statistics, accounting for 33 per cent of the workforce in 1960 and 29 per cent in 1970 (Massiah, 1986). These figures, of course, mark significant differences across territories, the range being as wide as 18–55 per cent in 1960 and 18–44 per cent in 1970 (Senior, 1991). Having said this, one must factor in the limitations of the tools used to determine participation in the labour force and economic activity generally. Massiah notes:

> The activities of women, though constituting work in the literal sense of the word, tend to be masked partly because they are often undertaken intermittently in the informal sector, partly because the income generated is so meager . . . and partly because much of the activity is undertaken in and around the house, the results being used directly for household maintenance.
>
> (Massiah, 1986: 183)

The emergence of Women's Affairs' Units within government

Another development, at policy level, was the establishment in the 1970s of 'national machineries' within governmental structures to deal with 'Women's Affairs'. These institutions were formed in the wake of the emergence of the new women's movement internationally; lobbying by local women's groups and especially women within the major political parties; and in recognition of the International

34

Women's Year and Decade declared by the United Nations. Of importance here is the establishment of two such institutions prior to the declaration of International Women's Year in 1975. These were the Council on the Affairs and Status of Women in Guyana (CAS-WIG) and the Women's Bureau of Jamaica, both established in 1973. According to Reddock and Tang Nain (forthcoming) Jamaica, in taking such action, became one of the first countries in the world to establish a Women's Bureau. In 1975, Trinidad and Tobago followed the pattern set by Guyana and Jamaica and established the National Commission on the Status of Women. Other territories in the region took similar action during the second half of the 1970s. Gordon (cited in Antrobus, 1988) has pointed to the limitations of these 'national machineries', noting that their main achievement has been in the area of sensitising the public and government bureaucracies to the welfare concerns of women. This statement, of course, generalises the achievements of these agencies, as some have been more dynamic and successful than others.

The re-emergence of the women's movement

Paralleling these developments at governmental level was the reactivation in the 1970s of the women's movement in the region, a trend that would increase in the 1980s. Women had observed that in spite of political independence and posturing about equality, they had remained marginal in terms of mainstream economic activity. This marginality was reflected in their concentration in a limited number of low-status, low-paying jobs, as well as in higher levels of unemployment and under-employment. One of the first organisations to be formed was the Caribbean Women's Association (CARIWA), which sought to link the various national coordinating councils to which many of the older women's organisations were affiliated (Reddock and Tang Nain, forthcoming). In 1977 significant collaboration took place between women's organisations in the governmental and the non-governmental sectors with the hosting of a meeting by the Jamaican Women's Bureau, CARIWA and the Caribbean Conference of Churches Women's Desk. This meeting was instrumental in the formation of the Women and Development Unit (WAND) of the University of the West Indies Extra-Mural Department (now School of Continuing Studies) in 1978, the Women and Development Programme of the United Nations Economic Commission for Latin America and the Caribbean (UN/ECLAC) in 1979–1980 and the

Women's Desk of the CARICOM Secretariat in 1980. Also in 1977, a feminist-oriented group – SISTREN Women's Theatre Collective of Jamaica – was formed, followed in 1979 by the formation of the Belize Organisation for Women and Development (BOWAND).

The 1960s and 1970s therefore represented growth and expansion in several areas, both governmental and non-governmental, and the emergence of a new consciousness among women about the discrimination and oppression they faced purely on the basis of being women. As the 1970s drew to a close the women's movement in the region stood on the threshold of strengthening its existence in an attempt to challenge age-old attitudes and institutions which had sought to keep women oppressed. Little did we know then, that the 1980s would produce new challenges which would threaten our practical gender needs and jeopardise the satisfaction of our strategic gender interests. Notwithstanding the controversial debate as to whether or not women, as a category, can have needs or interests in common, given significant differences of class, race, region, age and so on, I am here utilising Molyneux's (1985) and Young's (1988) theorising on the subject. According to their conceptualisation, practical gender needs refer to women's condition or material state, whereas strategic gender interests refer to women's position or their social and economic standing relative to men.

State retreat and structural adjustment programmes: the 1980s and 1990s

As stated earlier, a significant retreat of the state could be witnessed in this period, following its dominant role in the 1960s and 1970s. One of the main mechanisms through which the retreat occurred, with the possible exception of Guyana in the early stages, was the introduction of SAPs. Before discussing how SAPs and the retreat in general have impacted on women, I shall continue to highlight the development of the women's movement in the region.

The expansion of the women's movement continued apace with the formation, in Trinidad and Tobago, of Concerned Women for Social Progress (1981), the Group (1983) and Women Working for Social Progress – Workingwomen – (1985). The first two groups have since ceased to exist. Other groups include the Committee for the Development of Women in St Vincent and the Grenadines (1984); the Belize Rural Women's Association (1985); Sisi ni Dada in St Kitts/Nevis (1985); Red Thread Women's Development Project in Guyana

(1986); and the Women's Forum in Barbados (1989). These small, feminist-oriented groups focused on consciousness-raising among women, on articulating, publicly, the concerns and needs of women and on implementing various projects to address women's practical gender needs as well as their strategic gender interests. It is within this setting that CAFRA (the Caribbean Association for Feminist Research and Action) emerged in 1985, taking the bold step of defining itself as feminist. CAFRA is a network of individual feminists and women's organisations and its focus has been on research and action from a feminist perspective, as well as on networking. During this period, too, WAND underwent an ideological shift and began to utilise feminist theorising to challenge women's 'integration' into the dominant developmental model.

It will be observed, then, that at precisely the time when the women's movement in the region was expanding and strengthening – the early to mid-1980s – the retreat of the state (at least in Jamaica) was beginning. While the retreat has impacted on the movement, forcing some groups to focus more on women's practical gender needs rather than on their strategic gender interests, the existence of the movement along with the wider NGO movement has not allowed the retreat to go unchallenged.

The impact on women of SAPs and state retreat internationally

UNICEF studies were among the first to point to the differential impact of SAPs, noting that among the poor, the worst affected were women, children and the elderly. Other studies and writings from organisations such as DAWN (Development Alternatives with Women for a New Era), have pointed to the specific effects on women on account of their reproductive capability, and their gender-specific responsibility for reproducing labour-power through a combination of housework and childcare (Reddock and Tang Nain, forthcoming). A look at some specific sectors and strategies will illustrate the point.

The health sector

Because women tend to make more use of healthcare services than men, partly due to their biological role in reproduction, they are obviously more affected by what happens in this sector. For example, when cutbacks occur in these services, or when user charges are introduced or increased, or when such services are privatised (which inevitably means increased charges), it is women who suffer the most. Subsequently, such changes in the health services also affect women with respect to their social reproductive role. Sick children and adults may have to be hospitalised for shorter periods and thus women have to 'fill the gap' in terms of the extended periods of illness and recuperation (Tang Nain, 1992a). The other side of this coin is that since women predominate in terms of personnel employed within this sector, deterioration of buildings, facilities and other conditions of work also affects women disproportionately. We can recall here the case of Jamaica with respect to its health services and how recently, in Trinidad and Tobago, nurses were protesting against poor working conditions at the nation's main hospital.

Education

Here again women are more affected, both from the demand side and the supply side. From the demand side, increased pauperisation means that more students, generally, drop out from school or, due to decreased nutritional intakes, their performance levels suffer, as has already happened in Jamaica and Guyana. At the tertiary level, the introduction of taxes and increased fees will result in fewer persons receiving such education. The reason why women will suffer more is because data have shown that women need much higher qualifications than men to enter the labour market. With respect to Trinidad and Tobago, Reddock (1988: 499) notes,

> whereas in 1980, 67.2 per cent of males in the labour force had primary or no education only 48.1 per cent of females . . . were in this category. Similarly in 1980 whereas 28.6 per cent of males in the labour force had secondary education, it was 47.6 per cent of the females.

As far as the supply side goes, women's predominance in teaching means that they, like their colleagues in the healthcare sector, are more affected by deteriorating conditions.

Other sectors

While both women and men are affected by lack of housing and public transportation it is women, because of their responsibility (voluntary or otherwise) for children and the elderly, who are placed under greater stress. In the case of Guyana, the state's failure to provide potable water affects women far more significantly as here again, responsibility tends to fall on them to ensure that safe water is available in their households. This they achieve by seeking out safe water from springs, or by boiling or adding household bleach to the water received through their taps.

Income-reducing strategies

Here a range of measures has had severe repercussions for women. Wage cuts and retrenchment in the public sector affect women more adversely as, proportionately speaking, more employed women than employed men are concentrated in this sector, especially in the teaching and nursing professions. Figures for Trinidad and Tobago reveal that in 1981, 35 per cent of employed women worked in the public/state sector (it was 18 per cent in 1970). By 1991 the figure had dropped to 30.2 per cent. The introduction of value added tax (VAT), payable on all goods and services except food in unprocessed form, translates into poor women having to spend more time in the kitchen. Finally, other measures such as the reduction or discontinuation of subsidies on food and services, and the removal of price controls, serve to reduce real income in a situation where women earn less than men, and suffer higher rates of unemployment, and where many (up to 48 per cent in some territories in the Caribbean) are the sole breadwinners in their households. In practical terms this means going from shop to shop in search of 'cheaper' goods and it is invariably women who do the bulk of the shopping for their households. It could also mean reduced consumption of food, both quantitatively and qualitatively, and here again women are likely to be the ones worse affected as they strive to ensure that their children (and their men where applicable) continue to eat as well as is possible under the circumstances.

Writers such as Elson (1992) and others have pointed to the assumptions behind SAPs with respect to the infinite elasticity of women's labour. The *Financial Crimes* newspaper (August 1992) notes that women will get no sleep if IMF SAPs are to work, while others have suggested that the burden of the double day for women is now being increased to the triple day. Antrobus (1988), referring specifically to the impact of SAPs on women in Jamaica, points to increases in demands on their time as they are required not only to fill the gaps created by the diminished social services but also to find ways of increasing income to their households. It is within this context that poor women may seek employment in Export Processing Zones

(EPZs) where, in addition to receiving very meagre earnings, they face sub-standard working conditions, often in contravention of national labour laws.

The above discussion demonstrates that while macroeconomic policies and strategies are put forward as – and are assumed to be – gender-neutral, they often conceal a hidden gender bias with a resultant negative effect on women (Tang Nain, 1992b). Women's organisations (and other NGOs) have therefore been in the forefront of protests against SAPs. Women recognise that the strong state of the 1960s and 1970s was patriarchal (some feminists arguing that women had simply replaced dependence on individual men with dependence on the state), but the situation is appropriately summarised by Pateman as follows:

> There is one crucial difference between the construction of women as men's dependants and dependence on the welfare state. In the former case, each woman lives with the man on whose benevolence she depends; each woman is . . . in a chronic state of bribery and intimidation combined. In the welfare state, each woman receives what is her's by right, and she can, potentially, combine with other citizens to enforce her rightful claim.
>
> (Pateman, 1988: 256)

We look finally, then, at how the women's movement and the wider NGO movement have reacted to the retreat of the state and SAPs.

The response to SAPs and to the retreat of the state

Since the mid-1980s several NGOs, among them women's organisations such as CAFRA, SISTREN (Jamaica) and WAND, have not only criticised SAPs and the concomitant retreat of the state, but they have also called for a new development model which puts people first. The protests and pronouncements of these organisations have been aired at national, regional and international levels, and a successful campaign against the introduction of EPZs in Trinidad and Tobago was mounted by the local women's movement in the late 1980s. Future plans (of CAFRA and of the Women's Forum in Barbados) include research to determine in a more concrete way the impact on women of debt and structural adjustment.

One of the significant events which occurred during this period was a Regional Economic Conference in Trinidad and Tobago in

1991, hosted by CARICOM, to which the NGO movement was invited as a result of some lobbying.[5] Among the organisations invited were CAFRA, WAND, CCC and the newly formed (1991) Caribbean (NGO) Policy Development Centre (CPDC). CAFRA's three places at the conference were shared with Workingwomen of Trinidad and Tobago, and the Association of Women's Organisations of Jamaica (AWOJA). Having engaged in a process of preparation for the conference, the NGOs were able to produce a position paper which not only criticised the main conference document produced by CARICOM, but outlined, as well, the NGO perspective on development. Also, interventions were made on the various themes of the conference. The core argument of the NGO position was to reject the dominant economic model of development with its stress on the problem-solving capacity of market forces. As Antrobus (1992: 3) stated: 'The descendants of people who were once primary commodities in the world market have no reason to trust market forces with their lives!' The point was also made that one of the groups most exploited by the model are women, particularly in their unpaid work in the home and community, and in subsistence agriculture.

> We therefore need an alternative, more holistic, balanced model of development, one which can satisfy not only material needs but also the need for dignity, identity, . . . [and] which will allow us to maintain an harmonious and respectful relationship with each other, and with our natural environment.
>
> (ibid.: 5)

Later in 1991 the women's movement produced a paper at the invitation of the West Indian Commission. The paper's recommendations included calling on Caribbean governments to quantify women's work and to challenge IMF SAPs.[6]

In January 1992 Workingwomen (of Trinidad and Tobago) held a Women's Economic Conference which addressed, *inter alia*, the issue of debt and structural adjustment. Using the slogan 'Towards Constructive Adjustment', participants questioned why areas such as health, education and public investment in the economy, which were considered important to the state twenty years ago, had suddenly become unimportant. They asserted that the state ought to give the highest priority to the health and education of its citizens; that attention ought not to be given to the repayment of foreign debt to the exclusion of all other considerations, including the basic needs of citizens; that attempts be made to renegotiate and not simply reschedule the debt; and that consultation take place with citizens before incurring further debt.

The following quotation, taken from Joan French's presentation to the Regional Economic Conference, serves as an appropriate end to this chapter.[7]

> While the state needs to insist on the contribution of the private sector to the cost and delivery of social services, it is the primary responsibility of the state to ensure that the educational, health, social, recreational and reproductive needs of the population are met from birth to death at the level of factories, fields, the community and most importantly, the household. The state should set policy to ensure that the tradition of meeting these needs through the unpaid labour of women and the overextension of women's work time is broken. In this regard it is the duty of the state, by its policy, to break with the socialisation of females into roles which perpetuate their exploitation as the unpaid and over-worked reserve labour force onto which the responsibilities of the private sector and the state for the reproduction of the labour force are shifted, particularly in times of crisis.
>
> (French, 1992: 84)

NOTES

1 The English-speaking Caribbean, also referred to as the Anglophone or Commonwealth Caribbean, comprises the territories of Anguilla, Antigua and Barbuda, Barbados, The Bahamas, Belize, Dominica, Grenada, Guyana, Jamaica, Montserrat, St Christopher/Nevis, St Lucia, St Vincent and the Grenadines and Trinidad and Tobago, the majority of which are now independent states.
2 In the late 1980s the exchange rate was approximately J$5.00 to US$1.00. By 1992 it had reached J$26.00 to US$1.00.
3 A Goodwill and Fact-Finding Mission visited Guyana between 30 September and 5 October 1990. It was sponsored by the Caribbean Conference of Churches (CCC) and comprised economists, political scientists, international relations experts and theologians from the region.
4 By 1991 the official and street exchange rates had more or less equalized at G$125.00 to US$1.00.
5 CARICOM, or the Caribbean Community, was formed in 1973 to foster trade and greater cooperation between the states in the English-speaking Caribbean.

6 The West Indian Commission was set up by Caribbean governments to review and make recommendations regarding Caribbean development. It completed its task with the production of a report in 1992. The NGO movement commissioned a paper and held a consultation to critique the report.

7 Joan French is the current Coordinator of CPDC and a longstanding member of the women's movement in the region, having worked with both SISTREN (Jamaica) and CAFRA.

REFERENCES

Antrobus, Peggy (1988) 'The Situation of Women in the Caribbean: An Overview Including the Impact of Structural Adjustment Policies on Women'. Paper for UNDP/UNFA/INSTRAW Training Programme on Women and Development, INSTRAW, Santo Domingo, Dominican Republic, 28 Nov.–2 Dec.

—— (1992) 'Opening Session: Overview Perspective of Non-Governmental Organisations (NGOs)', in *Challenges in Caribbean Development: Interventions of Non-Governmental Organisations (NGOs)*, CARICOM Regional Economic Conference Feb. 1991, Caribbean Policy Development Centre, Bridgetown, Barbados.

Brown, Adlith (1981) 'Issues of Public Enterprise: Public Sector Issues in the Commonwealth Caribbean', special Issue of *Social and Economic Studies*, vol. 30, no. 1.

Caribbean Conference of Churches (CCC) (1990) *Official Report of a Goodwill and Fact-Finding Mission to Guyana, 30 Sept.–5 Oct.*

Elson, Diane (1992) 'From Survival Strategies to Transformation Strategies: Women's Needs and Structural Adjustment', in L. Beneria and S. Feldman (eds) *Unequal Burden: Economic Crises, Persistent Poverty and Women's Work*, Boulder, CO: Westview Press.

French, Joan (1992) 'The Role of Public and Private Sector Organisations and NGOs in Development', in *Challenges in Caribbean Development: Interventions of Non-Governmental Organisations (NGOs)*, CARICOM Regional Economic Conference Feb. 1991, Caribbean Policy Development Centre, Bridgetown, Barbados.

Henry, Ralph (1988) 'Jobs, Gender and Development Strategy in the Commonwealth Caribbean', in P. Mohammed and C. Shepherd (eds) *Gender in Caribbean Development*, Mona: University of the West Indies Women and Development Studies Project.

Levitt, Kari Polanyi (1990) 'Debt, Adjustment and Development: Looking to the 1990s'. Lecture, delivered at the Eighth Dr Eric Williams Memorial Lecture, Central Bank Auditorium, Port of Spain, Trinidad and Tobago, May 1990.

—— (1991) *The Origins and Consequences of Jamaica's Debt Crisis, 1970–1990*, Mona: Consortium Graduate School of Social Sciences, University of the West Indies/University of Guyana.

McAfee, Kathy (1991) *Storm Signals: Structural Adjustment and Development Alternatives in the Caribbean*, London: Zed Books.

Massiah, Joycelin (1985) 'The UN Decade for Women: Perspectives from the Commonwealth Caribbean', *Bulletin of Eastern Caribbean Affairs*, vol. 11, no. 2.

—— (1986) 'Work in the Lives of Caribbean Women', *Social and Economic Studies*, vol. 35, no. 2.

Molyneux, Maxine (1985) 'Mobilisation without Emancipation? Women's Interests, the State, and Revolution in Nicaragua', *Feminist Studies*, vol. 11, no. 2.

Moon, J. Donald (1988) 'The Moral Basis of the Democratic Welfare State', in Amy Gutmann (ed.) *Democracy and the Welfare State*, Princeton: Princeton University Press.

National Planning Commission of Trinidad and Tobago (1988) *Restructuring for Economic Independence: Draft Medium Term Macro Planning Framework 1989–1995.*

Pateman, Carole (1988) 'The Patriarchal Welfare State', in Amy Gutmann (ed.) *Democracy and the Welfare State*, Princeton: Princeton University Press.

Reddock, Rhoda (1984) 'Women, Labour and Struggle in Twentieth Century Trinidad and Tobago, 1898–1960'. Unpublished doctoral dissertation, University of Amsterdam.

—— (1988) 'Commentary: The Quality of Life', in Selwyn Ryan (ed.) *Trinidad and Tobago: The Independence Experience 1962–1987*, St Augustine, Trinidad: Institute of Social and Economic Research, University of the West Indies.

Reddock, Rhoda and Tang Nain, Gemma (forthcoming) '500 Years of Work and Struggle: Women's Socioeconomic Participation and Status in the Anglophone Caribbean 1492–1992', mimeo.

Senior, Olive (1991) *Working Miracles: Women's Lives in the English-speaking Caribbean*, Cave Hill, Barbados: Institute of Social and Economic Research, University of the West Indies.

Standing, Guy (1991) 'Structural Adjustment and Labour Market Policies: Towards Social Adjustment?', in Guy Standing and Victor Tokman (eds) *Towards Social Adjustment: Labour Market Issues in Structural Adjustment*, Geneva: International Labour Organisation.

Tang Nain, Gemma (1992a) 'The Impact of Prevalent Economic Strategies on Women's Lives in the English-speaking Caribbean and Women's Responses, With a Focus on Community Projects of an Economic Nature'. Paper presented at a Women and Development Seminar, Rio Predras, Puerto Rico.

—— (1992b) 'Economic Restructuring and Debt: A Gender Perspective'. Paper presented at a Teach-In on Equity and Sustainable Development, Toronto, Canada.

Walker, Alan (1984) *Social Planning: A Strategy for Socialist Welfare*, Oxford: Basil Blackwell.

Young, Kate (ed.) (1988) *Women and Economic Development: Local Regional and National Planning Strategies*, Berg/UNESCO.

4

INFORMAL SOCIAL SECURITY IN AFRICA FROM A GENDER PERSPECTIVE

Gudrun Lachenmann

INTRODUCTION

The present transformation processes in Africa can be characterised by the fact that there is no anchorage of structural adjustment programmes (SAPs) in society. This can be shown especially with regard to social policy and the evolution of gender relations. But rather than pose relevant questions in terms of the disengagement of the state, as suggested by the Introduction to this volume, I maintain that it is necessary to consider how social embeddedness of the economy has to be achieved, and who is the subject of social policy. This lies at the very heart of the relationship between civil society and the state. 'Social safety' and 'insecurity' are important components of this embeddedness (Lachenmann, 1993).

My diagnosis of the situation represents my response to the first of the two questions posed to the contributors of this volume, on the effects on women of insecurity-inducing global changes. This can be summarised by saying that a destabilisation of social and production systems has taken place in Africa, and that insecurity continues to increase during structural adjustment. This can be shown very clearly for women, whose established, but often invisible, social institutions of security are increasingly eroded. In this chapter, I make a special plea against labelling women as 'vulnerable groups', as is done in conventional structural adjustment discourses.

As a response to the second of the two questions, concerning women's responses to insecurity-inducing trends, I want to challenge the unquestioned notion that traditional forms of solidarity are breaking up as an inevitable consequence of the process of modernisation. The idea of formalising traditional solidarity and handing over all responsibility for social security to the state is neither realistic nor attractive. What is needed is the legal state alongside a maximum of autonomy on the lowest levels possible, pluralistic structures as opposed to monolithic solutions, as well as social movements for social control and creative forms of social change. The following methodological requisites of social policy would, in my opinion, lead to different solutions from what is considered to be the 'social dimension of structural adjustment' (SDA) (World Bank, 1990a):

1 consideration for actors, agency, strategies, processes, autonomy, institution building;
2 differentiation of levels, responsibility, subsidiarity;
3 emphasis on community instead of individualisation;
4 social policy understood as production orientation rather than social assistance;
5 self-organisation understood as autonomy rather than participation;
6 social security understood as strategies rather than static income levels and other quantitative indicators.

THE ANTI-WOMEN BIAS OF SDA

In this section I should like to discuss some areas where SDA is shown clearly to be inimical to elements of civil society, including institutions providing social security for women (see Gladwin, 1991). One of the most prominent features of structural adjustment discourse is the labelling of women as 'vulnerable groups', and presenting them as the target for all kinds of well-meaning poverty alleviation and social welfare measures (Lachenmann, 1988; 1992a). As a result of this, it is possible to disregard the adverse structural consequences for women's economy, as well as the unintended consequences of complementary sociopolitical measures. Through this labelling, women are rendered invisible as economic actors.

Women typically become recipients of marginal programmes which have very minimal financial resources. These programmes are, among others, small projects for women's organisations, and the famous income-generating projects through which the negative influences of economic decline, inflation, scarcity of resources and loss of markets become most evident. Beyond these, there are no serious efforts at adopting a more integrated approach combining subsistence production or reproduction work with market-oriented activities. On the contrary, studies carried out within the context of

SDA conclude that women should move to more efficient sectors in order to earn more (Haddad, 1991). Measures for human investment that emphasise the potential of women for further economic growth do not consider the processes through which women are increasingly losing the bases of their own economy and social security – important dimensions of their autonomy.

There is a vicious circle between women's loss of economic control of resources and their social position. As women lose control over economic resources, their social security dwindles as the 'traditional' rules of obligations and rights, reciprocity and solidarity are no longer valid, and relations of exchange and alliances are destroyed without alternatives emerging. The social embeddedness of the female economy changes: gender relations, division of labour, rights of access to productive resources, reciprocity. All this leads to an increasing work load and to a narrowing of the basis of female economy. For example, when women in West Africa cannot afford to pay for their daughters' dowries or to have capital for trade they are deprived of their own security, access to land and labour, and help from their kin in case of need. Their dependency on their husbands increases, while men fail in their obligations and, at the same time, patriarchal control over productive resources belonging to women frequently continues.

It is interesting to note that 'women-headed households' are the group considered to be a social problem. This fails to recognise not only that the 'normal' socioeconomic modernisation process is not taking place, but also that women may actually prefer to develop their own economy, with their children, in the absence of gender relations which include contributions by men. More generally, policy analysis and design do not consider important the relations which link women to different social groups, such as their family of origin. As a consequence, policies tend to affect such relations negatively, for example by the individualisation of farming systems, households and enterprises – which leaves no surplus for women to distribute, thereby destroying the basis of their security. Thus, the loss of security takes place through cutting off social bonds beyond the particular husband–wife relation. This is one dimension of what has been called 'house-wifisation' (von Werlhof, Mies and Bennholdt-Thomsen, 1983), namely, the dwindling of social embeddedness and the destruction of particular networks.

Neglect of 'unintended' socioeconomic consequences

Neglected, too, are the unintended consequences of structural adjustment with regard to access to productive resources, and the destruction of self-regulated activities. The dominance of efficiency-orientation according to 'modern' rules, results in the marginalisation of women living on subsistence production, who then become subjects of welfare interventions.

Also, the limited rationality of the policies included in the social dimension of adjustment has to be considered, as it is only income-oriented and not security-oriented. It does not provide room for change leading to the creative transformation of security-providing institutions, especially among the poorest and those living in rural areas. Because of this limited rationality, the cohesion of society is also destroyed. Examples of these types of policies include:

1 Public work schemes, which are only temporary in nature and which exclude women, though they still have to provide for the family. Participating men, on the other hand, tend to sell on the market the remuneration received in kind.

2 Early retirement schemes, for which women are hardly ever eligible as they normally do not hold permanent jobs as state officials. In addition, retired people move to villages and manage to appropriate, because of their relations and experience as former civil servants, valuable productive resources.

3 Private enterprise schemes that only touch very limited numbers of people and do not include technologically new branches. These, too, exclude women – either explicitly or as an unintended consequence of women not fulfilling criteria such as owning sufficient starting capital, or having adequate levels of education.

4 The crowding out of economic activities which are in general the domain of certain social groups, such as vegetable gardens dominated by young men instead of women, cereal trade taken over by male cooperatives in place of women.

5 Policies designed mostly for dynamic young men, who represent, of course, the highest political protest potential.

6 Policies that lack the budget necessary for recurrent costs in administration and which lead to further (informal) cost recovery – contrary to all ideas of deregulation.

Mobilisation of local resources and cost recovery

Contrary to what is assumed in the social policies of SAPs, in most countries there is no additional fundraising capacity, since none of the social services are really free. A great deal of cost recovery already takes place at the local level, in traditional or 'neo-traditional' forms. In fact, it is mostly women who collect this money (for water pipes, grain mills, health posts, etc.) and who carry out much of the so-called voluntary or self-help work for providing basic social security services (Bruchhaus, 1988).

It is unrealistic to assume that poor people or even those less poor could easily make out-of-pocket payments for services. In fact, it is the poorest who are frequently required to do so, while others have some insurance scheme on which to rely. Therefore, there is often a tripartite system of social services: private sector (including non-profit), (formal) social security, and public sector for the lower strata of the population. Furthermore, the more formalised new systems of social security become, the more mistrustful rural populations are likely to grow. This takes place within the context of considerable financial losses experienced, for example, by small savers in Benin, as formal banking institutions collapse.

'TRADITIONAL' FORMS OF SOCIAL SECURITY

The quest for security

The traditional 'social organisation of safety' in African societies can be characterised by generalised reciprocity and solidarity (Schott, 1988; Elwert, 1980; Elwert, Evers, Wilkens, 1983; Benda-Beckmann et al., 1988). However, 'tradition' as such is a myth, for there has always been change in social institutions and strategies. Certain 'traditional' principles, which were part and parcel of complex social and production systems and strategies, would be very useful in the 'modernisation' process but – according to my thesis – they are challenged by the destabilising processes of structural adjustment. Examples can be found in:

- coping capacities and strategies in drought periods in dry areas;
- flexibility and mobility in space and time;
- the system of 'sharing', which entitled women to certain supplies in kind (as remuneration or gift);
- systems of mutual help;

49

- forms of cooperation, for example between peasants and pastoralists, between allies in different regions and activities;
- diversified economic activities and strategies.

These are clearly opposed to the 'monoculture' of modernisation, with its individualisation of land ownership, restriction of mobility in space and orientation toward the economic efficiency of small enterprise/accumulation.

These 'traditional security' mechanisms are always based on diversification of production and division of labour, as well as on complex social relations, of which gender relations and female networks form a very important part. Women have their own security instruments – such as small-scale cattle holding, the gathering and sale of certain products, and, unfortunately, the sale of subsistence foodstuffs when necessary to satisfy other needs. These social and economic strategies of security are embedded in a system of solidarity, kinship, friendship, peer-groups and collective work for the needy. They try to restore the reproductive capacity of a unit, and are production-oriented rather than welfare-oriented in the narrow sense.

While contributions are often made in kind (including labour, or shares in the harvest), there is no fundamental contradiction with the monetarisation of social relations, although, of course, the latter may eventually break up the system because of the necessity to enter into the national market. It is also true that people with monetary income can afford to pay their social obligations in cash, for example to employ labourers, instead of participating in labour exchange. They might, therefore, start to profit more from these former relations, which eventually degrade into patron–client bonds. Even in this situation, informal security in health and education is available, via the support of urban relatives who take charge of more specific health events (e.g. surgery) or take care of education expenses. Similarly care, an important element of social security mainly provided for by women, is made available in the countryside to returnees and old people.

Clearly, the process of social differentiation is exaggerated by structural adjustment, and the insecurity and dependency of a large proportion of the population increase.

New 'informal' coping practices
The kind of social policy envisaged here is not a matter of second-best solutions, but it is essential to counteract the authoritarian system inherent in the prescription of the social dimension of structural adjustment. Also, it is not a matter of conserving traditional security practices, but of fostering creative, spontaneous, ever-evolving forms of coping with insecurity.

Old forms of traditional solidarity do not automatically dissolve with modernisation – new trends of self-organisation in industrialised countries show this. But current socioeconomic processes destroy old forms and prevent the establishing of new ones. In present times of crisis, the solidarity and sharing (such as borrowing from neighbours, etc. – 'one gets by') as well as caring for persons in need – over and above ordinary reproduction work – are mainly done by women. It is very often said that men give up in cases of distress. New networks are forming, for example women's groups such as those established within the context of the Presbyterian Church or self-help promotion organisations (such as INADES), or even an emerging peasant movement in Cameroon (Lachenmann, 1992c), which in addition to mutual help creates important space for the symbolic and spiritual strengthening of coping forces.

As opposed to official government–donor national food security programmes (which have been slowed down because of liberalisation), there are many new patterns elaborated at the grassroots level – namely peasant movements – in the field of food security. Where everybody knows that cereal prices are very insecure, there are village grain banks, which incorporate certain elements of traditional sharing, stock keeping, etc., but with different forms. Women take an active part, and have special schemes for providing basics such as soap and cooking oil in times of seasonal scarcity (such as pre-harvest). This means consumption credit, which normally is not provided for in modern credit schemes.

If drought and hardship become generalised, no possibilities of exchange are left, traditional stocks and reserves dwindle, and there are too many social obligations of sharing. Therefore, everybody is poor, irrespective of whether individual accumulation takes place. But even in these circumstances strategies are as numerous as ever, and people have the flexibility to take new chances. For example, in Senegal there are whole networks for collecting money and helping people to migrate, most recently to Italy. Again, in this kind of coping strategy, it is mostly women who contribute, but mostly women who are left behind – requiring new forms of social integration in the villages.

Everybody knows that savings clubs such as tontines become increasingly important, especially in a 'modern' environment. It is true, however, that many are very fragile and can exclude problematic cases from taking part, since the security margin is very low. It is also true that a contradiction between solidarity and credit–saving systems has recently been introduced. This is the case, for example, in the Senegalese peasant organisation which is now oriented toward accruing a profit for individuals (which, for spouses, of course, is better than it being oriented toward the household).

In Cameroon, where rotating credit associations and savings clubs are well established, women consider them to be their main support – not only financially but morally as well. Their purpose is the shared acquisition of necessary goods – nowadays much more than the so-called 'kitchen njangis' (communal kitchens) – as well as mutual aid. A recent study (Lachenmann, 1992c; Gsänger et al., 1992) which contributed to a generalised debate on the issue of security and development in the German context (Getubig and Schmidt, 1992), showed that amounts collected are usually very small. Despite this, it was clear from the research that women remained passionately committed to the tontines, to the extent that they became indebted to be able to pay their share, so as not to be excluded from the benefits.

Collective work in the fields – often considered to be a fundraising source for collective security – is nowadays quite problematic. The collective fields do constitute a tradition of repression and of dependency on personal relations. On the other hand, this important feature of mutual assistance was destroyed by collectivisation, and peasant organisations still follow the same practice.

Moneylenders are very important to social and productive security. They are often not (only) usurers, but represent important safety networks, as well as personal dependence. They still provide food when somebody is starving before the harvest.

Of course, it is difficult to step out of these patron–client relations because they guarantee survival, which no other relation does. Women in general are less creditworthy, and try to rely on relatives and neighbours for getting along in cases of need.

The forms of ownership and of mobilization for economic activities, such as cooperatives, are very important. In this context, the vastly complicated prescriptions for association of the population, through animation or community development, have been an intrinsic part of the recent authoritarian modes of governance. These have given the bureaucratic apparatus the means to control the peasantry, as well as to 'reinvent' traditions of communality. They have also brought the risk of new patriarchal relationships, through 'alternative' developmentalist notions. For example, it is known from experience in Mali that although these associations become more autonomous in the course of democratisation, women are excluded even more than they used to be by bureaucratic ideology, as is often the case with more formalised activities, be it in the economic, organisational or political fields.

Finally, there are new creative, flexible forms of collective economic activity, which have been able to gain an astonishing degree of freedom for manoeuvre, such as the so-called 'groupements à intérêt économique' (GIE) in Senegal, as well as non-governmental organisations. At present, however, they tend to combine the advantages of 'traditional' social relations (kinship ties, traditional access to land) with elements of uncontrolled capitalistic economy. It seems significant that in Senegal women's groups are in general not GIEs, but new legal forms are being developed which will again probably make them dependent. Why should women need special legal forms and not have their own autonomous groups with the same rights?

SOCIAL MOVEMENTS AND SOCIAL ORGANISATION FOR SECURITY

The potential of social movements

It is my opinion that social movements are the decisive societal force to develop creative new forms of social action, provide room for change, counteract the clientelist interlinkage of the political and economic system and overcome authoritarian modes of governance and the rigidity of the system. An example of one such movement will be given at the end of this chapter.

Women play a special part in social movements. In some countries, women are also able to influence politics accordingly, since, despite the absence of a recognisable women's movement, the importance of women's organisational efforts as an integrative factor combating insecurity is considerable.

Classical social movements such as post-independence liberation movements or trade unions, would in principle be the ones to promote adequate forms of self-help for social security. But they still have a very heavy historical legacy to undo. This is particularly so with regard to women, as they have been completely captured by the formal apparatus and are often regarded as representing merely their own interests. Also, the organisations (of youth, women) controlled by the one-party systems still generate considerable negative feelings, which will have to be overcome.

In West Africa, there are many different forms of social movements. In times of continuing crisis in the rural areas, and in the present process of formal democratisation and introduction of a multi-party system, their importance might decrease, or increasingly they might become an organisational focus of survival strategies. Voluntary and welfare associations have existed for a long time in West Africa. They represent new concepts of securing livelihood in changing environments, but follow 'traditional' patterns. There are also new ethnic movements that try to root mutual aid in ethnic orientations. Often the interesting feature is that these movements provide a linkage to the modern system, not in the form of patron–client relations, but with regard to the flow of resources.

Women have been known to take part in many historical protest movements. However, they are rarely represented at the higher levels of leadership, although their numerous participation is often used to create legitimacy for the developing state. In the frequent and enthusiastic literature on 'Africa on its way' (Pradervand, 1989) about self-help movements (for example, Naam and SixS in Burkina Faso and neighbouring countries), women's views are seldom mentioned. There are, however, many professional associations of women that are both pressure groups and typical self-help institutions providing social security in a broader sense. Lawyers', artisans' and nurses' associations are important examples. They also exist in the informal sector, where there are associations of women traders and hairdressers, for example in Nigeria. They constitute a kind of guild, exclusive and restrictive, which covers the main risks to production and livelihood. However, they struggle against repression, such as abusive fee collection by the police.

There are also peasant organisations that often assume the functions of local government, such as establishing and maintaining social infrastructure, for example, water management. Here, all problems of institutionalisation and professionalisation become relevant, in addition to the risks of being 'captured' by the state. In particular, it is often reported that as soon as women's projects are successful, the patriarchal structure appropriates them.

Solidarity, self-administration and responsibility should be present at the lowest possible level. However, the collective liability of peasant groups leads to the problem of levels of risk, to prevent the breakdown of the whole system. Here it is absolutely necessary to introduce autonomous funds for refinancing, on different levels, including guaranteed resource transfers from outside, such as foundations, while avoiding dependence on the international community's goodwill. In Senegal, women have insisted on having their own credit programmes, as they are more prepared to pay back their debts – even when they have to sell certain assets such as clothes or even jewels.

An important example of such solidarity and self-administration would be some kind of harvest insurance; when every third harvest falls below subsistence level (as is the case in many Sahelian countries), there ought to be a regular transfer with a simple distribution and allocation mechanism. Again, new appropriate forms might be autonomous foundations, which should be respected by governments. An example in Cameroon is a 'co-financing' programme of primary healthcare, organised on this basis.

Here the problem of subsistence logic comes into play for the women's economy, since the latter does not permit clear-cut distinctions between production and reproduction, credit for production and credit for consumption. Therefore, it is not feasible that such an economy should function according to generalised criteria of rentability, while 'the rest is social welfare'. The same applies to non-agricultural rural activities – which in their diversity form an important factor of security – and the informal sector. There are attempts in social movements to strengthen security-oriented 'subsistence' production, smaller, more flexible circuits, which are very often mostly supported by women. This means that financial contributions such as membership fees could be introduced, for example in health services (membership cards, etc.). This has been a long-established practice in NGO health systems (in initiatives supported by the churches), ensuring certain rights at the same time.

In principle, with decentralisation being taken seriously, local government should also have funds at its disposal for cases of emergency. The systems of 'indigénat' (assistance to indigenous needy people) still remain in some places, but given the present scarcity of public funds, no orderly administration of such funds can be expected and, as has been shown in the case of Cameroon, the small amounts available to the social welfare service have completely disappeared.

But the most important approach, in my opinion, would be to

organise social policy on the basis of professional activities, a variety of group memberships (regional, ethnic, cultural associations) and women such as market traders, school and parent groups.

The quest for security by a Senegalese peasant movement

I should like to complete this section with an example of the kind of social movement which I have been advocating. This was the subject of a study carried out in Senegal (Lachenmann et al., 1990). The highly developed Senegalese peasant movement had its precursors in self-help and youth groups, as well as women's groups organised locally in order to stop rural exodus. It gained momentum in the 1970s, when many groups were established for the purpose of channelling aid from international agencies in order to cope with famine during the big drought. In the main study area in Eastern Senegal – where the famine was not quite as severe as in other areas (except in 1984–1985) – the movement increased momentum by establishing collective institutions of food security (collective fields as well as granaries and cereal banks) and by improving general living conditions, especially through the supply of water. Since 1978, the movement has formed a national umbrella organisation which by 1989 claimed to have 200,000 active members, the majority of whom are women, thus covering approximately 1.5 million people.

In Senegal, NGOs are often characterised, rather deprecatingly, as providing more or less unprofessional but well-meaning help, useful for coping with the social problems of poor and minority groups, and as founded solely for the purpose of obtaining access to foreign finance. This means that neither their sociopolitical nor their economic role is acknowledged. In fact the Senegalese peasant movement has assumed an important economic role with regard to the main economic activity of the country (groundnut production and marketing), through a credit and savings programme established for inputs (mainly seed, since fertiliser has become too expensive). This lies at the very heart of a fundamental dilemma faced by the peasant movement, namely, having to stabilise the extremely fragile economic situation of the peasants, but thereby being forced to accommodate to the logic of the state-led economy and its old form of integration into the world market.

On the one hand, it is clear that this social movement is developing the possibility of negotiating the kinds of services people need. In the theory of social policy this would be called 'active client' and is an important aspect of interaction between state and society. On the other hand, however, there is the process of liberalisation and the reduction of state services (including agricultural extension) and subsidies on productive inputs (and basic consumer goods). Some peasants, mainly women, clearly see the importance of the credit and savings programme for securing their livelihood – providing them with seeds and small animals for their own farming. However, profits accrue to individuals, as credit is given and received by individual persons. Thus, it might be maintained that solidarity and generalised reciprocity are thereby destroyed and market logic introduced which in the end, given the economic situation, will not offer a secure living. But there also might be a chance to introduce new forms of collective economic logic and security, in other words a positive 'counter-modernisation', such as cereal banks, appropriate healthcare funds, harvest failure insurance, etc.

The peasant movement tries to stabilise food security (through millet prices and collective reserves), but mostly the situation of the peasants is such that they are not able to escape the debt trap. Diversification of production, contrary to the rhetoric, does not become effective, and irrigated vegetable gardening is overemphasised, taking on a largely symbolic significance.

Women bring in their 'traditional' forms of savings clubs (tontines), stressing that these are different from the formal savings and credit system which they consider too individualistic (which angers the leaders, who want to keep everything within the formal savings system). The women insist that it is important for them to do something together, to have some common activity. One could call it investing in new security-providing relations. Here an important integrative and security network is (re)constituted. In some marginal situations, the peasant organisation might provide the official framework for women to be active, for example by placing them 'under the protection of peasant leaders', especially in the groundnut basin, where men of working age have migrated. Also, women's group gatherings and feasts are evidently important to their own, female, identity.

This peasant movement – through its large female membership – is able to guarantee a certain social stability and establish new safety nets in a society characterised by extreme impoverishment and loss of social cohesion.

GUDRUN LACHENMANN

OPTIONS AND RISKS OF SOCIAL POLICY

Participation

In general, there is no social, economic or political participation in social policy in structural adjustment programmes. The tendency, on the contrary, is to finance contributions by paying for services, the quality and type of which cannot be influenced, supplied by professionals, and by an uncontrollable bureaucratic system.

For a long time now, participation has been identified as a self-help concept providing elements of social security. But participation has often been looked upon in the same way as forced labour in colonial times. There is a lot of enthusiasm for activities at the local level, but increasingly it is work that is forced upon people. And those who carry it out in the villages and peripheral urban centres are very often women. Here again, the contradictions are obvious. On the one hand, self-help is important in order to organise one's own life, so as not to become (self-)exploited, or pay an increasing amount for social services to an anonymous state. On the other hand, in most countries it is inconceivable that entire systems, for education, health, etc., could be financed at the lowest level by the poorest people. In this situation, it would probably be best, at least for the moment, if the state did not try to pursue cost recovery, but left revenues such as taxes in place at the lowest possible level. Then, both the social control of administration, through elements of civil society strengthened by associations, and social trust could be built up.

Individualisation versus community

The question posed at the beginning of this chapter was who is the subject of social policy or social security? In 'traditional' society, people are included in solidarity networks not as individuals, but on account of their – mostly ascribed – social positions. Nowadays, 'welfare' is calculated and attributed in terms of 'household', though it is recognised that intra-household distribution is not equal. This is very shortsighted in societies where each person, and especially women, increasingly creates their social position in a larger community and network (see, for example, Frey-Nakonz, 1984). These 'traditional' obligations cannot be met if market integration is total, especially when the rate of return is decreasing to the point of being negative – giving rise to the known

58

phenomenon of subsistence production (mainly female) subsidising market production.

The household (see Haddad, 1991) is too small an institution and its level is too low to guarantee generalised safety and security. The alternative should not be the state and anonymous security systems (which syphon away resources). Rather, it should be systems that are as uncomplicated as possible, which follow the subsidiarity principle *strictu sensu*: participation, power of decision making, self-administration and self-help, as opposed to professionalisation and bureaucratisation.

The principle of directing social policy to the individual, although linked to this subsidiarity principle, may have adverse consequences, such as destroying all kinds of social networks to which a person belongs because of her ascribed position. Only in cases of extreme individualised poverty and destitution should the public administration distribute funds, otherwise how would it be able to judge and control individual life situations without strengthening its authoritarian features? Only generalised old-age transfers might be a relatively simple policy measure. Even targeted measures on an unequivocal basis, for example to pregnant mothers or to feed children, lead to unintended consequences and ritualised services. This is because so-called modern social security transfers do not take into account social realities, for example they exclude other wives in polygynous families.

In summary, it is a fallacy to believe that modernisation necessarily leads to forms of individualisation. Rather, I am of the opinion that it is because of the type of 'modernisation' promoted by SAPs that the structural preconditions for responsible social security are absent. The insecurity of market integration is high, as is vulnerability due to reduced structural flexibility. Because of this 'individualisation' of persons, households or enterprises, no security margin is left for one's own survival or for helping others – what could be called solidarity capacity.

The welfare state illusion

It is important to look at certain contradictions which occur in the present situation when, because of the negative social impact of SA, a welfare state approach is advocated, and to consider arguments against its bureaucratic and patriarchal nature (see Schmidt, 1992; Gsänger et al., 1992). The dilemma can be summed up with Berger and Neuhaus

(1984), who state that there is a 'contradiction between wanting more government services and less government'.

This type of social-welfare oriented approach to social policy calls for more services, instead of trying to strengthen the autonomy of civil society in relation to the state. One argument against this attitude is that it is not viable, another that it will permit the 'capturing' of the population, meaning that it does not allow its autonomy and creativity. I refer to such phenomena as women being labelled by state services through authoritarian rituals of mother-and-child healthcare, which may lead to a loss of confidence in their own capacities as mothers and carers.

I believe also that it is an illusion to think that redistribution of resources to rural, poor or old and needy people will take place to any noticeable extent. Similarly, it is not seriously conceivable that, given the low level of resources, their reallocation to health and education will lead to more decentralised service delivery. Finally, talk of self-help and mobilisation is often just rhetoric to syphon off resources.

It is certainly misguided to think that the ideal situation is as much social services as possible; in industrialised countries alternative social movements have fought for freedom of choice with regard to the kind of social services in health and education, for example. It is important to struggle against professionalisation, medicalisation and being made passive objects of social services. Liberalisation, of course, carries the risk of pronounced elite formation and inequality, but also provides room for self-determination. There is certainly also the risk of social stratification: the rich will have private insurance and services, those employed in the formal sector and represented by trade unions will have social security, and those working in the informal sector, including women, will be left to a state system which is not at all free.

Official social security schemes for the formal employment sector are also not very promising for women. This is because women are more often employed in insecure jobs, and do not fulfil the necessary conditions for receiving transfers. Also, those formal social security schemes recently discussed in relation to those not employed in the formal sector hardly touch women. For example, in Cameroon the International Labour Organisation (BIT, 1989) elaborated a proposal to extend formal social security to the non-salaried population. After much consideration it recommended a system for small peasants reached by the parastatal marketing boards for coffee and cocoa. The peasants were supposed to pay 'equal shares' for monthly contributions covering health services (in state institutions) for a family of up to nine persons. However, in the meantime, world market prices for these cash crops have fallen drastically and the parastatals have been dissolved. Even if the programme had been implemented, it is clear that only export cash-crop producing men would have been considered. This would have been the case even though in Cameroon, as is well known, women are or used to be (men are now moving into food production) completely independent agricultural producers. Furthermore, the calculations made for possible contributions (11 per cent of cash-crop income) – on the basis of income surveys – considered all health expenses to be available for the formal contribution, but did not provide at all for necessary expenses for private or informal social services.

INTERACTION BETWEEN STATE AND CIVIL SOCIETY

Social safety by non-governmental organisations

According to Glagow (1989: 34) 'market failures and similar shortcomings of the state in solving given social problems draw the political and theoretical attention to something else beyond markets and the state'. He stresses the 'capacity of this "third sector" in fulfilling societal demands which cannot be adequately satisfied by markets and/or the state' (see also Anheier and Seibel, 1990). Here, as in the development discourse in general, this third sector is discussed with regard to the fulfilment of basic needs. I think another important line of argument is the role of the third sector as a societal force which decisively constitutes the space where social rights are located and social control is executed; in short, where self-organisation takes place. Frequently, this aspect of social power (Lachenmann, 1992b) is neglected and only the fulfilment of basic needs through NGOs is considered.

One of the main issues is the articulation between 'traditional' forms of reciprocity and exchange and new creative forms which constitute the 'third sector' and which, as elements of civil society, would be able to interact with the state. Of course, there is always an invisible form of articulation, and very often, especially for women's institutions, it is preferable not to formalise linkages because of unequal relations (leading to the syphoning off of resources).

61

However, in the long run it seems important to formalise and make autonomous these third-sector institutions.

Certain types of formalisation might be interesting, as they show signs of seriously changing the character of the institutions. For example in Cameroon, it is true that the cooperative sector totally excludes women (with the exception of some women's palm oil cooperatives). But there are new approaches: there are organisations of employees for social events, cooperative credit unions which develop special desks for women's groups (in North West Cameroon) and include a kind of life insurance, and there are community-based forms of credit and saving. Certain banks are preparing, together with self-help promotion organisations, to appropriate these models in order to provide the rural population with access to formal credit. Here, the well-known risk is, on the one side, the exclusion of women, and, on the other side, the monetarisation of people's socioeconomic activities and thereby the destruction of their safety networks.

Although one should not be too optimistic, there is a clear movement oriented towards different social organisations which do not follow official state-imposed patterns for the rural population. Nevertheless, all the possible critiques apply about being too dependent on external resources, and reinforcing and perpetuating patriarchal modes of organisation as well as charismatic leadership. But it should be recognised that there are attempts to transform the former authoritarian and development approaches, as well as attempts at the creative evolution of existing forms of cooperation.

It is also important to realise that structuring on higher levels also takes place, namely on the intermediate level of so-called self-help promotion organisations, as well as on the inter-regional level through networking. Thereby, new forms of knowledge formation and models of self-administration have been initiated, which are highly relevant to safety issues. Here it becomes especially clear that the 'developmentalist' discourse has been too rigorously oriented towards increases in productivity, and did not include the ways economic activities are embedded in the economy.

Until very recently, the international donor community focused almost exclusively on 'the grassroots level'. I would call this the technocratic or welfare approach instead of the empowerment approach. Now (World Bank, 1990c) the link has been made between these 'grassroots' and government and state, thus taking into account, although implicitly, social structure and power relations. Hyden (1990: 43) characterises intermediary, non-governmental organisations as 'key institutional actors' because they give support to those parts of the population who do not receive it from formal ones. They provide incentives, including technical advice, and build management capacity in communities. Hyden rightly states that the 'notion of institutional autonomy' barely exists in Africa, and should be strengthened. He stresses that the economy has to be deregulated and, at the same time, points out that 'private and public institutions that sustain a market economy must be strengthened'. Hyden (ibid.: 73, 51ff.) also points out that 'development is not only a matter of economic outputs and social services but the creation of viable structures of governance that involve the private and voluntary sectors as much as the public one', including 'diversification of institutional responsibility for societal action'.

CONCLUSION

The above implies that the legal state has to be strengthened so that it can fulfil its role of guaranteeing the necessary environment for a moral economy and social and civil rights. The decisive issue is the social negotiation of gender relations. The crucial question here is who commands the resources at which level of authority in society, and who has the power of definition of social problems? This is no call for an authoritarian welfare state but, as Hyden (1990) puts it, for an 'enabling environment'.

Therefore, the main issue in social policy under conditions of adjustment is the balance between the social responsibility of the state, with its dangers of bureaucratisation, on one side, and the multiple actors in civil society for bringing about autonomous social security, with its dangers of self-exploitation, on the other.

Most importantly, social policy should not syphon off resources, but rather place financial autonomy at the level where resources are mobilised. In addition to autonomy, a plurality of possible solutions should be achieved through horizontal communication networks.

SAP policies can only be successful if they are able to counteract the 'insecurity' and the destabilising aspects of the economy, for example world market prices. This does not mean that one should oppose liberalisation and economic rates of returns. Yet how can security of livelihood be guaranteed if production inputs become so expensive (after reduction of subsidies) that there is no return – which especially is the case with women's activities? Therefore, these policies should take sustainable development seriously with regard to securing production systems – and consider sustainable development also at the level of the social and production systems. Instead of formal social security schemes, security of economic conditions and access to resources are needed in order to enable people to go on caring for themselves and for their relatives, and to provide for their old-age security. One might speak of social sustainability.

At present, SDA policies are not at all oriented towards 'capacity building' (World Bank, 1990b). This is not a question of discretionary economic policy, but of collective political action, to stabilise prices, to control the agricultural banking system, in other words to introduce a different 'moral' economy. It is not 'traditional' economy and social structure that are insecure, but the way the 'modern' system has developed.

Protection has to take place not in the sense of opposing market principles, but of strengthening actors in the market. This, of course, can include new forms of segregated, local markets and non-anonymous and non-monetarised social relations – typical of women's economic activities and work.

Women in Development (WID) policies are being taken seriously in Africa (Lachenmann, 1989), I think mainly because of their accidental character, not having achieved institutionalisation and inclusion on a policy level (Staudt, 1990). But there has been no sustainability in any of the programmes, including those of SDA. Instead, their character becomes more and more social (Buvinić, 1986), as SDA rhetoric continues to talk of the vulnerability of women and to lack coordination. Furthermore, SDA measures are very rarely actually implemented. Unlike the position taken by the Commonwealth Expert Group (Commonwealth Secretariat, 1989), I do not think it is very helpful to call for more and more exact data on the impact of SAPs on women. We already know a lot – it is now a matter of listening and acting.

REFERENCES

Anheier, H. K. and Seibel, W. (eds) (1990) *The Third Sector: Comparative Studies of Non-profit Organisations*, Berlin and New York: Walter de Gruyter.

Benda-Beckmann, F. von, Benda-Beckmann, K. von, Casino, E., Hirtz, F., Woodman, G. R. and Zacher, H. F. (eds) (1988) *Between Kinship and the State: Social Security and the Law in Developing Countries*, Dordrecht: Foris Publications.

Berger, P. L. and Neuhaus, R-. J. (1984) 'To Empower People', in D. C.

Korten and R. Klaus (eds) *People-centered Development: Contributions toward Theory and Planning Frameworks*, West Hartford, Conn.: Kumarian.

BIT (Bureau International du Travail) (1989) 'Rapport du Gouvernement de la Republique Camerounaise sur l'Extension de la Protection Sociale aux Populations Non-salariees', Geneva (OIT/TF/CAMEROUN/R:13).

Bruchhaus, E. M. (1988) 'Frauenselbsthilfegruppen: Schlüssel zur Entwicklung aus Eigener Kraft oder Mobilisierung der Letzten Reserve?', *Peripherie* 8, 30–31: 49–61.

Buvinić, M. (1986) 'Projects for Women in the Third World: Explaining their Misbehaviour', *World Development* 14, 5: 653–664.

Commonwealth Secretariat (1989) *Engendering Adjustment for the 1990s: Report of a Commonwealth Group on Women and Structural Adjustment*, London: Commonwealth Secretariat Publications.

Elwert, G. (1980) 'Die Elemente der Traditionellen Solidarität', *Kölner Zeitschrift für Soziologie und Sozialpsychologie* 32, 4: 681–704.

Elwert, G., Evers, H.-D. and Wilkens, W. (1983) 'Die Suche Nach Sicherheit: Kombinierte Produktionsformen im Sogenannten Informellen Sektor', *Zeitschrift für Soziologie* 12, 4: 281–296.

Frey-Nakonz, R. (1984) *Vom Prestige zum Profit: Zwei Fallstudien aus Südbenin zur Integration der Frauen in die Marktwirtschaft*, Saarbrücken and Fort Lauderdale: Breitenbach.

Getubig, I. P. and Schmidt, S. (eds) (1992) *Rethinking Social Security: Reaching Out to the Poor*, Kuala Lumpur and Eschborn: Asian and Pacific Development Centre and Deutsche Gesellschaft für Technische Zusammenarbeit.

Gladwin, C. H. (1991) 'Introduction', in C. H. Gladwin *Structural Adjustment and African Women Farmers*, Gainesville: University of Florida Press.

Glagow, M. (1989) 'The Role of NGOs in Development Aid', in L. Bekemans, M. Glagow and J. Moon, *Beyond Market and State: Alternative Approaches to Meeting Societal Demands*, San Domenico: European University Institute, Working Paper 89–140: 33–69.

Gsänger et al. (1992) *Beyond Traditional Solidarity: Self-help and Social Security in Rural Pakistan*, Berlin: German Development Institute.

Haddad, L. (1991) 'Gender and Poverty in Ghana: A Descriptive Analysis of Selected Outcomes and Processes', in S. Joekes and N. Kabeer (eds) *Researching the Household: Methodological and Empirical Issues*, IDS Bulletin 22, 1.

Hyden, G. (1990) 'The Changing Context of Institutional Development in Sub-Saharan Africa: Creating and Enabling Environment', in *The Long Term Perspective Study of Sub-Saharan Africa*, background papers vol. 3: *Institutional and Sociopolitical Issues*, Washington, DC: World Bank.

Lachenmann, G. (1988) 'The Social Problems of Structural Adjustment Policies in Africa', *Economics*, A Biannual Collection of Recent German Contributions to the Field of Economic Science, 32: 74–96.

—— (1989) *Frauenpolitik in der Entwicklungspolitik. Verbesserung der Rahmenbedingungen für Frauenförderung in Afrika durch Entwicklungszusammenarbeit*, Berlin: German Development Institute.

—— (1992a) 'Frauen als gesellschaftliche Kraft im Sozialen Wandel in Afrika', *Peripherie* 12, 47–48: 74–93.

—— (1992b) *Social Movements and Civil Society in West Africa*, Berlin: German Development Institute.

—— (1992c) *Die Gefährdung Sozialer Sicherung in der Krise und Perspektiven neuer Strategien der Selbstorganisation: Fall Kamerun*, Berlin: German Development Institute.

—— (1993) *Selbstoranisation sozialer Sichernehit von Fraun in Entwicklungslandern*, University of Bielefeld, Sociology of Development Research Centre, Working Paper 191.

Lachenmann, G., von Bechtolsheim, M., Becker, S., Karakurt, T., Melick, J. and Pragua, C. (1990) *Organisations paysannes au Sénégal: comment renforcer les structures intermédiaires dans le processus de transformation socio-économique*, Berlin: German Development Institute.

Pradervand, P. (1989) *Une Afrique an marche: La Revolution silencieuse des paysans Africains*, Paris: Plon.

Schmidt, S. (1992) 'Social Security in Developing Countries: Basic Tenets and Fields of State Intervention', in I. P. Getubig and S. Schmidt (eds) *Rethinking Social Security: Reaching Out to the Poor*, Kuala Lumpur and Eschborn: Asian and Pacific Development Centre and Deutsche Gesellschaft für technische Zusammenarbeit.

Schott, R. (1988) 'Traditional Systems of Social Security and their Present-day Crisis in West Africa', in F. von Benda-Beckman et al. (eds) *Between Kinship and the State: Social Security and the Law in Developing Countries*, Dordrecht: Foris Publications.

Staudt, K. (1990) 'Gender Politics in Bureaucracy: Theoretical Issues in Comparative Perspective'; 'Context and Politics in the Gendered Bureaucratic Mire', in K. Staudt (ed.) *Women, International Development and Politics: The Bureaucratic Mire*, Philadelphia: Temple University Press.

von Werlhof, C., Mies, M. and Bernhaldt-Thomsen, V. (1983) *Frauen, die letzte kolonie,* Rowohlt: Reinbek bei Hamburg.

World Bank (1990a) *Analysis Plans for Understanding the Social Dimensions of Adjustment*, Report 8691-AFR, SDA Unit Africa Region.

——(1990b) *Making Adjustment Work for the Poor: A Framework for Policy Reform in Africa*, Washington, DC: World Bank.

——(1990c) *The Long-term Perspective Study of Sub-Saharan Africa*, background papers vol. 3: *Institutional and Sociopolitical Issues*, Washington, DC: World Bank.

5

IN SICKNESS AND IN HEALTH

Gender Issues in Health Policy and their
Implications for Development in the 1990s

Jo Beall

INTRODUCTION

The enjoyment of good health is at the root of personal well-being
and security, in the short and long term. A gender perspective on
health is one which recognises this for women as well as men.
Women have specific health needs arising out of their biological role
in reproduction, as well as their tasks and responsibilities within the
gender division of labour in any particular sociocultural context. In
addition, however, a gender[1] perspective in healthcare starts from
the premise that there are biological and social synergies between
the health of children and that of their parents – particularly
mothers but also fathers – which provide a compelling rationale
for integrating a *gender* perspective into mainstream health policy
and practice.

There is often a confusion between the issue of women's health and
that of engendering healthcare. By seeking conceptual clarity in
relation to health policy, this chapter addresses the frustrations of
practitioners and planners in the health sector who are frequently
exhorted to 'take account of gender issues' and who invariably reply
'why?' and 'how?', given their perception that women's health already
receives a significant or even disproportionate allocation of healthcare
attention and budgets. Health personnel in Third World countries
assert that gender issues are being dealt with because women's health
needs are taken care of through the preventative strategies of primary
healthcare (PHC) programmes or through targeted vertical pro-

grammes such as maternal and child health (MCH) and family planning (FP).

However, women and particularly poor women are addressed by policymakers largely in their roles as mothers and wives through programmes with an obstetric and paediatric bias. Often seen as conduits to husbands and children and targeted in promotional and educational campaigns, women's own health concerns outside of their reproductive role and childbearing years are frequently overlooked. Although shifts in health policy have led to obvious and immediate benefits for many women, both as recipients of care and as carers, access to curative healthcare has remained difficult for them.

Gender relations in society and the household mean that men generally have greater access to and control over resources. They are more likely to consume resources and therefore to command treatment. However, in the context of increasingly limited resources for health expenditure in many countries, an emphasis on vertical programmes and selective primary healthcare (SPHC) and the focus on health education within PHC which is invariably targeted at women, men's access to preventative healthcare is recurrently neglected. This has implications for their own well-being as well as that of their households.

Thus, a key argument of this chapter is that gender relations in society and gender stereotyping in health policy and planning skew access to healthcare along gender lines. There is a concomitant danger that men are ignored by promotional and preventive programmes, and women are denied curative care outside their reproductive role. Engendering health policy for development in the 1990s implies responding to the needs of both women and men, in sickness and in health.

The health sector, perhaps more than any other, has been concerned to target women. However, this has not always meant it has addressed women's health needs and rights. The sector has found it particularly difficult to incorporate a gender approach into its policy perspectives, its research practice and the planning and management of health delivery systems. This chapter explores some of the reasons for this in relation to the impact of health policy on low-income men and women in the Third World, as it has evolved under changing development policy approaches over recent decades.

DYNAMIC AND STATIC TENDENCIES IN POLICY

In order to highlight some of the different forces that can influence policy processes, this chapter presents a broad historical analysis of health policy over recent decades. The analysis helps to address the questions posed in the Introduction to this volume, and especially the issue of how shifts in policy, here specifically for the health sector, impact on well-being and security.

Policy is defined as decision-making processes and deliberate actions by public institutions (for example governments, donor agencies, NGOs, political parties and organised interest-based groups) seeking to promote development and address conditions or problems they identify as important (Wuyts et al., 1992). Issues reach the wider policy agenda when pivotal, organised groups in society wish to see change or improvement. Policy is thus over-determined by political power holders and those to whom they owe their position or allegiance.

However, policy can also be influenced by those it is meant to serve, by those who implement it, and by organised interest-based groups who wish to change it and take up an advocacy role on particular issues, or who lobby through research and its dissemination. The political force of women, organised and acting in different ways in various contexts, has had a significant impact on policy at certain times. However, their policy clout has been subject to insecurity because hard-won gains can be quickly overturned when competing with stronger interests, particularly in conditions of resource scarcity and economic exigency. For instance, women's participation in national liberation struggles has won them short-run gains, but these have not often been sustained in the post-independence period (Beall et al., 1989). This phenomenon is nowhere more evident than in the case of social policy, given its redistributive potential and the political dimensions involved. Moreover, given women's comparative disadvantage in terms of political power, it has been difficult for them to influence policymaking towards meeting their interests in a sustained way. This is evidenced in cases as diverse as in the United Kingdom where women have lost the material gains afforded by the welfare state, and in Cuba. There women benefited in policy terms from the peace dividend which included nationalised land and capital, but their gains were undermined by economic adjustments and an increased emphasis on productivity (Nazzari, 1983).

The policy process

Policy changes are never completely new. Fresh ideas and innovations, in health as in any other sector, often emerge out of the failures or inadequacies of past approaches. They are introduced and implemented in the context of legacies from the past, as well as current conditions. Such legacies, which can be political, institutional or attitudinal, affect the potential for change, which in turn is often resisted. Thus, policies are built on or are a reaction to preceding priorities and orientations and are determined by the institutional framework of policy. Policy combines an accrual of attitudes and solutions to past problems with the introduction of new goals and new solutions on the policy agenda. It is this which has encouraged women themselves to be instrumental in inserting their issues into the policy context, for example demanding reproductive rights, and which leads to instrumentality on the part of policymakers with regard to women-focused policy, for example population programmes and family planning projects.

Despite these constraints posed by existing power relations and institutional frameworks, the ongoing importance of advocacy and campaigning organisations promoting health issues and women's health rights cannot be overestimated. Single issue campaigns and interest-based groups working in the health sector articulate user demands and priorities in relation to health and serve to hold health professionals and planners to account. They are vital to the goals of empowerment and equity in health because they are often concerned to advance women's strategic gender interests (Molyneux, 1985).

However, there is also a need to encourage on the supply side, gender awareness and competence on the part of decision makers, professionals and practitioners engaged in the formulation and implementation of health policy. This is necessary in order that they can respond to the priorities of different users which are gendered, and recognise the immediate and practical gender needs of women and men (Moser, 1989).

A gender perspective on health would include a 'diagnosis' of the situation of and relations between women and men and their resulting health priorities, understood both in terms of rights and needs. It would ensure 'consultation', involving representatives of women and men users and of male and female health workers in decision-making processes concerned with prioritisation in the delivery of healthcare. A gender perspective in health planning would facilitate the integration of the different concerns of women and men into the 'treatment and management' of healthcare. This in turn requires that health research and health planning procedures are informed by an approach where data (for example, target groups and research populations) are disaggregated on the basis of gender.

Recognising difference on the basis of gender relations does not necessarily insinuate separate, vertical health programmes for women. When these have been fought for and achieved, they have frequently been subject to instrumentality by governments and donors, for example with family planning services becoming less to do with reproductive choice and more to do with population control. It implies rather, a cross-cutting approach which requires a reorientation of attitudes through gender analysis, as well as the development of practical skills and 'gender competence' both for those involved in policymaking and those at the forefront of healthcare delivery. Rather than constituting a once-and-for-all exercise, engendering health policy is a process, an incremental process based on the introduction of fresh perspectives and the pragmatic identification of feasible means and entry points for adaptation and change.

DEVELOPMENT PARADIGMS AND THE EVOLUTION OF HEALTH POLICY

This and following sections of the chapter examine the evolution of policy approaches to development as they have influenced and affected health policy, while shifts in relation to women and gender are traced. Women were not a particular focus of policy before the 1970s, and until the 1980s the emphasis was primarily on women rather than gender. This focus largely derived from the political impact of the women's movement and women's organisations, networks and NGOs, as well as the growth of the women in development (WID) lobby within donor agencies and national governments. Women tended to be viewed in isolation from their relations with men until a gender relations approach provided such contextualisation (Whitehead, 1979; Young et al., 1981) and sought to understand policy in these terms (Beall et al., 1989; Kabeer, 1991; 1992a). It is only more recently, however, that effort has been made to seek ways of under-standing and integrating gender in terms of the policy mainstream (Johan, 1992; Levy, 1992; Kabeer, 1992b).

Shifts in health policy cannot be said to directly parallel changes in wider approaches to development. However, neither has health policy been free of their influence. It is possible, therefore, to illustrate trends in health policy which have shadowed not only the paradigmatic shifts in development, but also the associated approaches to women and gender which have accompanied them.

Health policy is never considered or acted upon in isolation. A glance at the 1990 World Development Report (World Bank, 1990) shows that defence budgets exceeded the percentage devoted to health in all but nine middle- and low-income countries and since the 1970s the percentage spent on health has been going down rather than up. Moreover, the impact of economic crisis and reform has been the subject of a number of recent investigations of the relationship between macroeconomic adjustment and healthcare (Genberg, 1992; Pinstrup-Anderson, 1992; WHO, 1992b). Thus health policies are pursued within the context of other policy frameworks which can enhance, undermine or contradict their aims. Social policy more generally is particularly vulnerable and subject to insecurity in times of economic stress. Among the social sectors, however, health fares relatively well. This is partly because public health provision forms an important part of many political platforms and manifestos, and partly because a number of key health statistics, such as infant mortality rate (IMR), maternal mortality rate (MMR) and life expectancy are used as indicators of a country's overall level of development. Despite this, in competition with other ministries, health ministries are often weak and ineffective in delivering an appropriate level of care. They encounter perennial planning and management problems, dealing as they do with people often in conditions or times of extreme vulnerability, and as they address the most intimate and personal aspects of people's lives, coming face to face with firmly held socio-cultural beliefs and practices.

Health policy has gone through several mutations both internationally and nationally. Changing perspectives and priorities in health are contextualised and presented more or less chronologically, although it is important to bear in mind that they are not historically discrete. Right up to the present, within global strategies, national policy frameworks, sectoral programmes and individual projects, it is possible to find a number of orientations operating coterminously. The influence of successive legacies for current efforts to effect broad-based and equitable healthcare delivery systems is examined, highlighting the gender dimensions and implications involved.

THE LEGACY OF HEALTH HIERARCHIES AND 'DISEASE PALACES'

Those countries which, through necessity or choice, opted for a market economy after independence, adopted an accelerated growth model in pursuit of economic development. It was believed that rapid indus- trialisation, mechanisation of agriculture and investment in large- scale infrastructure would generate rapid economic growth. The creation of wage employment on a large scale and the drawing of 'surplus' labour from the rural subsistence sector would increase cash incomes and overall demand for goods and services. This, in turn, would provide further stimulus to the expansion of the modern wage economy. The development of the market was seen to play a key role in the process, with the benefits of growth 'trickling down' to all. Despite the importance accorded to the market, the accelerated growth model nevertheless involved a considerable degree of govern- ment intervention in the economy.

Macroeconomic planning by the state was not accompanied by the same degree of social planning. The residual model of social welfare that simultaneously prevailed, held that government intervention to meet social needs should be kept to a minimum as living standards and welfare would be improved through economic growth. Intro- duced by colonial authorities, the residual model operated on the basis that social needs would be met through individual effort and the family. Expenditure on social services was deemed non-productive and a drain on national resources that could otherwise be directed at expanding the modern industrial economy. Thus, social welfare confined its responsibilities to social deviants and those 'vulnerable groups' who could not engage in the market economy and who were not supported by the family or charitable and voluntary organisations. Informing the accelerated growth model was modernisation theory, which saw development as a series of progressive changes through which societies would be transformed from traditional to modern, industrialised states (Hardiman and Midgley, 1982).

In line with this approach, health policies and medical services were modelled on those of the industrial nations where health was defined as 'the absence of disease'. Under colonialism, curative medicine and hospital-based treatment were prioritised, catering primarily for the colonialists and the better-off urban-based indigenous population, or those within reach of mission hospitals. Towards the end of the colonial period, there was a growing concern with the spread of

73

communicable diseases, and public health measures such as immunisation were introduced.

Following independence, this model persisted, involving vast expenditure on sophisticated hospitals with specialised facilities, high salaries for Western-trained professional staff and imported technical equipment and pharmaceutical products. Modern medical schools became symbols of national prestige, and self-care and customary health practitioners which had hitherto served most health needs, and continued to do so for the bulk of the poor and rural populations, were eschewed. Separately managed immunisation campaigns coincided with this model, through top-down, vertical programmes aimed at specific objectives. And, indeed, astonishing accomplishments were achieved in the near elimination of some dreaded diseases such as smallpox.

Despite considerable shifts and advances in health policy since the 1950s and 1960s the legacy of this period persists, with a large proportion of governments' public health resources being consumed by the high costs of centralised, curative medical services and with multilateral assistance agencies investing heavily in eradication programmes. Despite macroeconomic pressures, most governments in sub-Saharan Africa continue to regard public health expenditures as a priority. However, examination of the distribution of the health budget among types of services suggests that the bulk of expenditure goes to hospitals and non-essential drugs rather than to basic health services (Pinstrup-Anderson, 1992).

A gender critique of health policy under modernisation

If we disaggregate the modernisation approach on the basis of gender, we find that it was mainly men who were addressed in the context of economic growth, both as contributors and as beneficiaries. They alone were valued as producers and workers. It was men who benefited from jobs, acquisition of skills, training and education, as well as healthcare and insurance for those in secure and formal employment. It was assumed that the household was a corporate unit, headed by a male householder whose gradually increasing assets and resources would be equally shared with other household members.

Women were treated as passive beneficiaries of development and in terms of healthcare their own needs were largely ignored. To the extent that they were addressed at all, it was in their role as wives and mothers. Hence, mothers were targeted as conduits to children in immunisation programmes. The assumption was that if women were assisted in catering for the health, welfare and nutritional needs of their families, the overall interests of the household would be served. However, while women's responsibility for meeting the routine healthcare needs of their families was relied upon as a resource, it was not valued. For example, their worth as repositories of customary knowledge and wisdom about local disease prevention and cure went unacknowledged.

Thus, to the extent that public health provision was seen as a necessary part of investment in human capital, this did not extend to the majority. Curative healthcare through the private or public sector was out of the reach of most people, both women and men. Preventive measures, however top-down they were during this period, did alleviate the burden of healthcare for communicable diseases, carried largely by women within the household. However, they left unattended the underlying causes for poor health deriving from poverty, powerlessness and a changing environment. Moreover, along with modernisation came the detrimental effects of Western innovation such as increased and new forms of poverty, environmental degradation and the widespread emergence of Western diseases such as those related to alcohol and tobacco consumption.

THE LEGACY OF REDISTRIBUTION WITH GROWTH AND ALMA ATA

Although the strategies based on modernisation and an accelerated growth model were initially successful in economic terms during the First UN Development Decade (1960–1969), there was increasing evidence of spreading distress and new forms of poverty. The paradox of apparent wealth and growing indigence, manifest in over-populated rural areas and concentrations of urban poor in burgeoning informal settlements, was clearly not a temporary phenomenon. The recognition that the majority of the population were not benefiting from the accelerated growth model led to a shift in thinking which stressed redistribution as a prerequisite for continued economic development.

Redistribution with growth advocated a poverty-oriented approach which targeted the poor by giving them access to employment and productive resources to improve their income. It was thought that this would increase mass purchasing power and raise demand for basic goods and services which would in turn foster growth. Labour intensive strategies were advocated, especially in agriculture, and the recognised inability of the formal sector to absorb the supply of labour, focused attention on facilitating the informal economy. Rapid population growth was identified as an important cause of poverty, or as responsible for eroding efforts to address it. Associated with redistribution with growth was a concern with meeting basic needs. There were those needs which it was believed could be met through individual effort – such as the need for food, shelter and clothing – and those needs which required public provision – such as health, sanitation, water and education. Thus, large areas of social policy in this context relied heavily on policy prescription and state provision and planning.

Primary healthcare

In the spirit of basic needs, at the 1978 Alma Ata conference the World Health Organisation (WHO), together with the United Nations Children's Fund (UNICEF), declared their goal of universal primary healthcare, a goal which it was believed could be achieved by the year 2000. As a critique of the failure of existing hierarchical, vertical, curative and high-tech healthcare models to serve the health needs of the majority of people, a wide-ranging and process-oriented model of primary healthcare (PHC) was offered as an alternative.

Through comprehensive and horizontal provision, PHC was defined as a mixture of promotional, preventative, curative and rehabilitative activities of a basic nature, which would involve people in the determination and delivery of their own healthcare needs. It was holistic in its approach to health, which was defined as 'a state of physical, mental and social well-being'. This was to be achieved through the combined activities of extended basic health services, intersectoral cooperation and community development. These activities together included education about health problems and their control; the provision of safe water and basic sanitation; immunisation against major infectious diseases; appropriate treatment of common diseases and injuries; provision of essential drugs and the integration of vertical maternal and child health (MCH) and family planning (FP) programmes into horizontal programmes (Phillips, 1990).

Primary healthcare remains the dominant objective or approach to health problems in most developing countries and continues to be promoted by the international health community as the best hope of ameliorating if not solving the health problems faced. And yet as the year 2000 approaches, the noble goals of PHC are far from having been reached, with steady population growth fast eroding gains which are made.

The most successful efforts at PHC have been small-scale projects and programmes. Difficulties arise when there are attempts at replication and scaling-up, and with the administrative and managerial shifts required when changing from vertical to horizontal service delivery. On the supply side, there are often financial problems leading to excessive dependence on donor support, with inevitable implications for sustainability and conditionality. Political problems include lack of commitment to PHC on the part of leaders who continue to favour the more visible hierarchical and hospital-oriented approach. There are also practical problems of delivery, including a lack of appropriate personnel and managerial competence, particularly within the lower echelons of the system. On the demand side, PHC is often regarded as the inferior offering of a two-tier health system, a palliative to which low-income communities are required to contribute, by a social system which places scant value on the health of the poor.

A gender critique of redistribution with growth and primary healthcare

The shifts in development thinking in the 1970s were paralleled by different efforts to link women's issues to development for the first time. First were those who highlighted women's contribution to the economy and their role as active participants in development and who demanded equity in policy and planning. Second were those who made the link between poverty and population growth, making women firm targets of development policy.

Together, these trends formed different thrusts of what has become known as the 'women in development' or WID approach to development policy. It gained institutional form with the advent of the UN Decade for Women (1975–1985) and the setting up of women's desks in development agencies and of women's bureaux or ministries in the government structures of many developing countries. Within this context there were two main policy thrusts in respect of women, one which emphasised gender equity, and one which emphasised improving the position of poor women (Moser, 1989).

Those who had as their goal the redistribution of resources from men to women and who were concerned with women's rights found less ready acceptance in international agencies and national governments than those with a poverty focus. They emphasised legal and political equality, the right to equal economic participation and reward and the right of women to have their reproductive role valued and accommodated by policy, for example through equal opportunities legislation. In terms of health policy, the influence of this approach can be seen most readily in the struggles of women's organisations, NGOs and health coalitions to advance women's strategic gender interests. It took the form of asserting women's right to healthcare not only during childbearing and lactation but throughout their lives, and calls for reproductive freedom and women's control over their own fertility.

Ideally, the equity goals of WID and those embodied in PHC might have intersected, but they did not. The reasons for this are many – the comparative political weakness of the women's lobby, the strength of other vested interests, the instrumental use of women and women's programmes to pursue different objectives such as population control and child development, the failure of institutionalised WID to meaningfully connect with the lived reality of many Third World women, and the inability or unwillingness of policymakers to take the equity agenda of WID seriously.

Moreover, despite the equity objectives of Alma Ata, the orientation of PHC fitted more comfortably with the poverty alleviation approach which came to dominate the 1970s and which largely confined redistribution with growth to a concern with basic needs. Poverty alleviation strategies were less challenging than calls for gender equity. Here, women's poverty was linked to underdevelopment rather than gender subordination, and was seen as a product of past failures to acknowledge women's contribution to development (Moser, 1989).

Women's role both in the economy and in providing for their families' basic needs was recognised and they became a critical target group in development. Objectives were to improve their access to employment, enhance their productivity through access to productive resources and to increase their access to contraception and family planning. In line with this approach, as well as its intrinsic aim to reach poor communities, PHC addressed women specifically, both as recipients and as providers of healthcare.

PHC and women's health needs

Ideals and intentions aside, in terms of delivery it is difficult to generalise about the implementation and effectiveness of PHC programmes. They have changed over time and differ from one context to another. They differ in terms of institutions involved and initiating activities, focus and means. However, to the extent that the effectiveness of PHC has depended on gaining entry into and acceptance by communities, and on mobilising them through health workers drawn from their ranks, initiators and managers quickly came to appreciate the value of women as healthcarers and of women's collective organisation for access.

Women were specifically targeted as users by PHC, notably through MCH and through promotional components such as educational campaigns in health, hygiene and nutrition. Despite this emphasis on women, PHC has not always succeeded in meeting their health needs and has not addressed the issue of rights. Success stories are often confined to particular projects or regional programmes, but in terms of examples of best practice, there have been practical advantages for women as the primary carers within the household and community. They have benefited as carers, for example, through improved environmental conditions and through programmes aimed at eradication of specific diseases such as immunisation and oral rehydration therapy (ORT). Targeted components of PHC, such as MCH, FP and under-five clinics have also had positive practical effects. However, many benefits have been achieved at the expense of women who are required to spend time, energy and resources on PHC activities and solutions, often at expense to themselves.

There have been conflicting aims within the practice of PHC as well. On the one hand, there is the goal of holistic and comprehensive healthcare which is at the same time promotional, preventative, curative and rehabilitative. On the other hand, there is pressure to improve specific development indicators such as the infant and maternal mortality rates, notably through family planning. When seen through the prism of gender, this highlights contradictory rather than complementary policy objectives. In the first case the goal is the total well-being of children and men and women at all stages of their life-cycle. In the second case it is to promote mother and child health at certain points and in particular roles.

This can be seen through the operation of MCH, FP and under-five clinics, which are invariably conducted within single and separate programmes. Although it was envisaged that they would be part of a horizontal delivery system, in practice they are often run vertically, through separately organised and managed centres. These are usually supported by donors who dictate priorities. Obstetric care is consistently given precedence over gynaecology and many have asked 'where is the M in MCH?' Girls aged six and upwards are not eligible for care at MCH centres until they become mothers themselves and elderly women have little or no recourse to care (Smyke, 1991). Moreover, the combined delivery of MCH and FP has served to render concerns such as infertility a non-issue, and has excluded men from provision of and information about contraception. This fails to acknowledge men as important decision makers in sexual and reproductive health. The combination of obstetric care and family planning objectives in single clinics can lead to a mixing of missions by over-zealous health personnel.

Thus, despite some undeniable practical benefits, PHC has fallen short of its original equity objectives. It could be argued that the disproportionate focus in PHC on paediatric and maternal health has served to exclude the health needs of much of the adult population – women outside of their childbearing role, and men. Moreover, the inability of PHC to consistently and effectively deliver curative and rehabilitative care, constitutes a failure to address the social as well as the biomedical synergies in parental and child health. For example, one of the greatest causes of households descending into poverty is the death or disability of an adult male breadwinner, affecting not only the worker but dependants as well (Harriss, 1989).

PHC and women as healthcare providers

It is the case that women are everywhere disproportionately represented within the lower echelons of the healthcare hierarchy as providers. This is reflected within PHC as well. Women in the community have played a key role in horizontal PHC programmes, often giving freely of their time and energy, particularly when efforts have included community participation, for example in integrated approaches such as improvements in sanitation and clean water supply. PHC has also placed considerable reliance on community health workers (CHWs) or village health workers (VHWs) who are used as paid or unpaid animators, educators or health aides, and women have often been the target of recruitment drives.

In trying to explain the lack of success of many PHC programmes, problems commonly identified are the failure to adequately integrate PHC into district health systems, problems of intersectoral cooperation, poor selection, training, support and supervision of CHWs and their wretched working conditions and remuneration (Phillips, 1990). A gender critique points to the necessity of disaggregating this analysis on the basis of gender.

Given the pivotal role women are expected to play in PHC as CHWs and VHWs it is necessary to question the preconceptions and social relations which have ensured that when there is remuneration and training men are often to be found among the VHWs and CHWs. Women, on the other hand, are usually found when VHWs and CHWs are engaged as 'volunteers' or for minimal pay (often in kind). They, in turn, are often neglected in terms of training and support. It is the case that in good PHC programmes women CHWs and VHWs can derive from their work, skills, income and status in both their households and communities. There is the potential for empowerment when they are also involved in decision-making processes in relation to the development of PHC. However, while this might be the case in particular projects, it does not seem a generalised experience. It has been observed that it is often men who are put forward for the better paid and trained positions and who swell the ranks of the Community or Village Health Committees with whom decisions often rest (Raikes, 1992).

In this sense, therefore, PHC has done little to challenge gender relations, either through genuinely involving women workers in decision-making processes or through significantly enhancing their skills, remuneration or status. This goes a long way towards explaining organisational and management problems if the context is one in which a significant proportion of the healthcare providers have been excluded from participation in the system in a meaningful way; where women have been expected to provide time and energy in the community over and above already burdensome demands in the household and in jobs; where it has been assumed they would do this for minimum returns; and where there have been few role models of their own sex in better positions to fuel their aspirations.

THE LEGACY OF ECONOMIC REFORM AND STRUCTURAL ADJUSTMENT

The 1980s saw a deteriorating economic situation in the industrialised market economies and increased indebtedness in developing countries. Together with high debt repayment and lack of investment capital, developing countries had to cope with falling demand and lower prices for their basic export commodities. The 1980s also witnessed a dramatic upheaval in ideas about development, sufficiently drastic to have been called a 'counter-revolution' (Toye, 1987). Its theorists questioned that development should be led by governments at all, and proposed market deregulation, privatisation and a reduction in the size and scope of the public sector. Hence, the recommended solutions for ailing Third World economies were stabilisation and structural adjustment policies which included cutbacks in state activity and public expenditure, loosening of controls over production and trade, and encouragement through incentives of private entrepreneurship.

By the 1980s, the contribution of women to development was being recognised with greater clarity and enthusiasm. In the interests of economic efficiency, efforts were made to harness women's economic participation on the understanding that to fail to do so would be to under-utilise a valuable economic resource (Moser, 1989). However, the result frequently has been the use of women as development solutions, to increase the effectiveness of development interventions, rather than to accord them any agency.

Not only on the demand side, but on the supply side as well, women in the 1980s were forced to increase their labour force participation in many countries, given the rise in prices of most basic goods and the fall in real household income. Thus, women have played an important role in relieving the negative effects of adjustment policies at the household level, through greater labour force participation and informal sector activities. Adjustment policies have also compelled women to engage in a variety of individual and collective survival strategies and to participate in the provision of basic services in the community. Reductions in state expenditure on public goods and services, including healthcare, and the introduction of user charges have increased women's domestic burden. The unspoken assumption and the reality is that the extra work created will be taken up by women and their daughters (Elson, 1989). Thus, the impact of economic crisis on healthcare has been to increase the cost of public healthcare and to shift the burden of care on to communities and individual households, with differential effects for women and men.

Economic reform measures and IMF and World Bank conditions for adjustment have generally entailed a reduction in budgetary proportions spent on the social sectors, although there are variations with regard to health depending on whether governments see themselves as politically committed to public provision of healthcare (Pinstrup-Anderson, 1992). Nevertheless, by the late 1980s, many donors had begun requiring the introduction of some kind of cost recovery in healthcare as a condition for supporting healthcare programmes.

Cost recovery and targeting in health

In 1987 the World Bank published *Financing Health Services in Developing Countries: An Agenda for Reform* (World Bank, 1987), which argued that curative healthcare should be paid for as a marketable commodity, while public health measures such as sanitation, safe water and waste disposal, and preventative programmes such as immunisation, would have to be organised and financed by the state and communities themselves, given that the benefits extended beyond actual recipients. Further exceptions were allowed in the case of preventative care for mothers and children and those unable to pay due to poverty. The underlying assumption was that the production, distribution and consumption of health services were 'analogous to those of any other commodity' and that fees should be charged unless market failure could be shown to exist (Bloom, 1991).

The same year, UNICEF proposed the 'Bamako Initiative' which suggested that problems of healthcare and drug supply in Africa could be solved by cost recovery. The initiative proposed charging for essential drugs, including those used in MCH and in the GOBI system (Growth monitoring, ORT, Breast-feeding and Immunisations), and in the GOBI/FFF (family planning, food production and female literacy), with the proceeds going to revolving funds to repurchase drugs and as income for local PHC and MCH initiatives. Thereafter, UNICEF issued operational guidelines for the Bamako Initiative which have been widely endorsed by a number of African countries (Phillips, 1990).

The recommendations and implications of these two initiatives fed into existing debates within the health sector itself. The first concerned a debate about the potential of PHC to provide comprehensive healthcare, a debate which preceded the crises of the 1980s. Despite the goals of Alma Ata it was clear that for many countries, inadequate funding and personnel and organisational bottlenecks in the provision of essential health services would persist. This led some to argue for assigning priorities, and to advocate selective primary healthcare (SPHC) which recommended effective use of scarce resources to tackle conditions which could be treated or averted effectively and at the least cost. SPHC typically focuses on paediatric conditions such as measles, whooping cough and neo-natal tetanus, and embraces ORT in the treatment of gastro-intestinal diseases.

Critics of SPHC argue that it 'places relative costs on human lives' and that 'the complex poverty syndrome of malnutrition, gastro-enteric diseases and respiratory infection will not yield to specific programmes' which are often vertical and in any case divorced from more comprehensive PHC initiatives (Phillips, 1990). In effect, however, the impact of adjustment and the associated erosion of resources for healthcare have helped nudge SPHC out of the realm of debate, so that selective interventions at the expense of comprehensive healthcare in many contexts have become the order of the day.

The 'Bamako Initiative' also raised important ethical questions which fed into a second and even older debate between those who advocate a health service financed and provided by the state and those who favour a free market in healthcare, with means testing for those who cannot afford to pay. The weight of economic reform has led to an evaluation of ability to pay replacing the criterion of need in healthcare. Rather than the issue of targeting itself being problematised, discussion is confined to who should be targeted for relief, and how this might best be effected. This is in spite of many political manifestos guaranteeing free healthcare provision, and the equity principles enshrined in Alma Ata.

The gender dimensions of affordability and 'willingness to pay'

Cost recovery in healthcare need not necessarily impact adversely on poor people, for example, if revenues generated from user charges imposed on the better off (such as private patients and those with private health insurance) are used to maintain effective healthcare provision for the poor. However, means testing and transfers carry with them a number of difficulties. Targeting is both complex to manage and costly to administer, and cannot guarantee that poor people's access to healthcare will not be adversely affected by cost recovery. Moreover, it seems that targeting is gender-biased towards women and has served to marginalise men in terms of access to public or subsidised healthcare. This may be appropriate targeting but it serves to reinforce, once again, women's entry to health provision on the basis of their being a 'vulnerable group', or by virtue of their role as mothers and carers. Illustrative of this is the list of official exemptions from the user fee system in Jamaican public hospitals – visits for family planning, immunisations, women with high-risk pregnancies, food aid recipients, children in uniforms and pensioners (Lewis and Parker, 1991).

If not disaggregated on the basis of gender, studies which seek to identify households' ability and 'willingness to pay' for healthcare will not reveal the context-specific gender relations which influence who in a household will get access to healthcare under a user fee system. For example, in many West African countries men and women have separate areas of financial responsibility and are customarily responsible for different areas of household expenditure. This needs to be taken into account when assessing a household's ability to meet health costs (Orubuloye et al., 1991; Welbourn, 1992), for it is quite possible that a man expresses 'willingness to pay' for family healthcare when it falls into the realm of the woman's budget. In South Asia, the introduction of user charges has articulated with existing gender relations, reinforcing son-preference in accessing healthcare (Ostergaard, 1992). It has forced women in low-income households in many countries to choose between decreasing their own use of health services or finding extra cash through reduced consumption or increased work (Raikes, 1992; Welbourn, 1992).

Evidence from India points to the negative effects of women's increased employment on child survival, measured at the extreme by the level of childhood mortality (Basu and Basu, 1991). Harriss (1989) suggests for South Asia that ill-health is the most important factor pushing people into poverty and destitution, particularly when the person sick is the adult wage earner. Frequently, household assets as well as income are utilised in the purchase of curative care, often in the private sector. The survival of public sector healthcare is often at the expense of a reduction in the extent and quality of service, particularly for curative care. This has led to a significant shift towards use of the informal sector in the form of traditional healers, semi-legal practitioners and self-care (Raikes, 1992). A recent study in Zambia (Forsberg et al., 1993) found that visits to traditional healers were more expensive than government health services, and yet accounted for more than 80 per cent of total health expenses of the group surveyed. This same study, along with others (Lewis and Parker, 1991; Genberg, 1992), concludes that affordability is not an insurmoun-

table obstacle to the introduction of user fees, in spite of noting that
'There was no difference between expenditure on adults (K92 per
visit) and children less than five (K91), while there was a substantial
difference in expenses on illness in men (K149) and women (K43)'.

ENGENDERING HEALTH POLICY
TO THE YEAR 2000

Where does this multiple legacy leave us in the 1990s and what, if
anything, is new? The pessimistic answer is that the legacy is one
which bequeaths more problems than it solves and that the 1990s offer
little promise for the millennium. An optimistic response would be to
build on the positive aspects of what has been inherited, and to seek
new openings. In relation to health policy itself, it is possible to
identify specific opportunities in the shifting priorities and emphases
in the health sector, notably in the areas of reproductive health,
environmental health and health planning and management. Engendering health policy in the 1990s involves working creatively with
existing policy legacies to identify constraints, opportunities and
room for manoeuvre. Room for manoeuvre exists in translating the
language of development policy into progressive and gender-sensitive
policy and practice.

Human development

There are opportunities in the current language of human development and the linking of poverty and productivity at the wider policy
level, for example in the human development approach being promoted by the multilateral agencies (UNDP Human Development
Reports, 1990 onwards). The emphasis on social development and
human creativity, for example, represents something of a shift from
the exclusive focus on economic efficiency which characterised the
1980s. Once development is seen as being about people, rather than
factors of production or units of labour, for example, it is a step closer
to recognising that those people are men and women.

Admittedly, *human development* as understood and articulated by
some institutions can easily get translated solely into a preoccupation
with human resource investment. And for health policy governed by
ongoing macroeconomic trends, this can result in viewing the health
sector solely as the welfare arm in economic recovery (Kabeer and
Raikes, 1992). In gender terms, this could reinforce the preoccupation

86

with paediatric and obstetric health. Nevertheless, the human development rhetoric provides a benchmark against which public action can pit itself, whether it emanates from the endeavour of health advocacy groups, international agencies concerned to promote social policy and combat poverty, or national governments wishing to preserve an element of state responsibility for healthcare.

Sexual and reproductive health: involving women and men

The current shift in focus from family planning to sexual and reproductive health encourages a recognition that women have health needs in relation to sexual activity beyond childbearing and brings in men as sexual actors and as partners in reproduction. The cynical view might be that it is only the emergence of HIV and Aids as a major preoccupation of health policy that has prompted the shift of family programmes from MCH clinics into other horizontal healthcare structures. It is difficult to quantify or measure the impact of ideas. However, that would be to devalue decades of effort and struggle by women themselves for health rights and reproductive freedom, both within the development and health arenas. Moreover, it would be to fail to capitalise on the opportunities these shifts present, for integrating a gender perspective into mainstream health policy and care.

The Safe Motherhood Initiative, launched in February 1987 by WHO and supported by a number of UN and bilateral agencies as well as many NGOs, has helped put the 'M' back into MCH. Some argue that little has been achieved in real terms in improving conditions for women and that men are still free of responsibility in terms of reproductive health. Moreover, it can be argued that Safe Motherhood merely represents a concern for improving maternal mortality indicators which are used to assess the level of a country's development and its commitment to redistribution. However, it also represents a genuine concern on the part of many policymakers and practitioners to prevent death in childbirth and constitutes an advance in meeting women's reproductive health needs.

Gender dimensions in environmental health

The environmental lobby's focus on sustainable development can provide an important entry point for engendering the health sector. Efforts to consider *people* as part of ecology have been important towards engendering the sustainability perspective in development. The introduction of the idea of social sustainability owes much to the women and gender lobbies in development, for if account is not taken of the multiple responsibilities and needs of women and men and the way these have to be balanced on a day-to-day and generational basis, development interventions cannot hope to be either participatory or sustainable.

The increasing focus on environmental health can also have positive effects in encouraging the health sector to recognise gender differences. For example, water supply improvement – which is a fundamental component of PHC – has had obvious benefits for women and there are increasing efforts to involve women in local discussions and decisions on water supply development, previously a male preserve. The fact that women are the ones who primarily work in and with water, means that they are more susceptible to parasitic infections such as schistosomiasis (bilharzia), which is transmitted through freshwater snails which thrive in rivers, lakes and dams. A gender perspective has improved recognition of this, and the relationship between the effects of schistosomiasis such as anaemia, and other sex-specific factors of women's health such as menstruation, frequent pregnancies, malnutrition and exposure to malaria and intestinal parasites (personal communication, Nordberg, 1993).

Gender issues have also been taken into account in relation to injuries and violence which are becoming an increasingly important part of mortality and morbidity patterns in many countries. Many injuries are gender-related in ways that are sometimes simple and sometimes very complex: occupational accidents are different for women and men depending on the nature of their work; traffic injuries affect men more than women, while domestic burns and poisonings affect mainly women. Violence affects women and men in different ways, both in its nature and where it takes place. The fact that understandings such as these are taking root within the health sector in turn serves as a catalyst for extending gender awareness further.

Planning and managing health delivery with a gender perspective

The 1990s are witnessing a concern to improve the planning and management of healthcare delivery. The prospects are poor given the decline in public health services at all levels, crumbling facilities, the poor pay and de-skilling of health workers through lack of training and support, and the consequent low morale. While decentralisation offers no panacea for more effective and equitable healthcare delivery and certainly carries no intrinsic benefits in terms of gender equity, support to health planning and management associated with restructuring of healthcare delivery can provide opportunities. An important entry point is human resource development and training which can include the development of gender awareness and gender competence among health planners and health workers.

Health planners and workers, frustrated in their efforts to incorporate a gender perspective, need to be provided with the competence and tools to do this. At a practical planning level, an example would be the collection of gender disaggregated statistics to help assess the different health patterns and needs of women and men. Although these are collected at the point of delivery, figures are often aggregated once they are entered onto tally sheets by health personnel. Merely to require health workers to fill in more columns in order to keep sex-disaggregated statistics is not the answer. This constitutes extra work for already demoralised and overworked staff, and returns may not be accurate unless this requirement is accompanied by an involvement of staff in decision making and a process of training so they can appreciate the importance of the activity.

At the level of research, another important entry point is to ensure gender disaggregation in utilisation studies which are important in informing health planning and management. While time, distance and cost are variables that are normally measured for impact on the use made by recipients of various forms of health provision, the different access of women and men to such resources is not. It is particularly important to understand, for example, the opportunity costs of attending different types of healthcare for low-income women who have to perform a variety of different responsibilities and balance tight and diminishing budgets.

Empowerment for equity in health

Finally and importantly from the perspective of policy as public action, among Third World women themselves there has been a focus on organisation and empowerment of women in development – DAWN: Development Alternatives with Women for a New Era (Sen and Grown, 1988). This approach, which emerged in the late 1970s, is primarily a response to, rather than a part of, mainstream development. It emphasises the notion of women's self-reliance and sees women as furthering their interests through collective and bottom-up mobilisation around their practical and immediate needs. It places as much weight on the process of struggle as on its outcome in assisting women to overcome their disadvantages, in getting access to and control over resources, and in deriving a place in decision-making fora.

In relation to healthcare, both in the Third World and the industrialised countries of the North, an empowerment approach has encouraged and supported women in a variety of self-help activities, including gaining and developing their knowledge of health problems and treatment. This approach has challenged the patriarchal and hierarchical nature of medicalised healthcare, the expectation that patients should play a passive role in their own treatment, the cheerful dismissal of many female complaints, control over access to contraceptive advice and fertility treatment, and the negative side-effects of certain kinds of modern medical treatment. However, to date such initiatives have been disparate and unstructured and have failed to impact significantly at the policy level through publicly agreed and stated goals. Neither is it clear that such an approach has resonance with all women's perceptions of health and their healthcare needs, some remaining uncritical of doctors and health systems and resistant to taking responsibility for their own health.

Healthcare is often expressed as a priority by low-income men as well as women. However, there are fewer examples of men organising around their perceived health needs. It is difficult, therefore, to ascertain what their gendered health interests might be. In the industrialised countries there is evidence of some men acting collectively in relation to treatment of HIV and Aids, and globally there are many examples of men in trade unions including among their concerns occupational health issues. But for most men healthcare is less central to their involvement in public action than it is for women, unless they work or are engaged in medical or health professional structures. This needs to be understood if men's gendered needs are to be elicited and addressed by policy as public action.

Democratising and engendering the health policy process has to include working with women and men, for change on both sides of the politics/policy interface. As suggested in the section above on 'Dynamic and static tendencies in policy', the role of campaigning and advocacy organisations is important for working to change policy frameworks and perspectives. However, empowerment in respect of health cannot be confined to self-help initiatives. A society also needs funded, organised and planned health services, both for the sick and for the healthy. Empowerment in health might include assistance in achieving proficiency and skill in self-care. But it should also include support for the efforts of women and men to identify and articulate their healthcare priorities, both within and in tandem to conventional health delivery systems.

Consultation and participatory planning skills are required to elicit the interests and expertise of men and women users. In practical terms, this means both looking to see where women and men are in society – in what occupations, in what locations, how they interact with their physical and social environment – and listening in different ways for the voices of those who are silent, rather than taking silence for acquiescence or ignorance and deciding on their behalf. This approach would be entirely compatible with the current development goals of 'decentralisation', 'consultation', 'participation', 'partnership', 'enablement' and 'choice'.

To achieve consultation and participation it is also important to promote gender awareness and develop gender competence on the part of those working within the health sector at various levels, either as policymakers, planners or practitioners, so that they too are empowered in their professional work. Such an approach should be seen as a complement to, rather than an alternative for, continued efforts on the political and advocacy fronts. Without the will and the ability on the part of those formulating and implementing health policy, the efforts of health campaigners will never see the light of day. Engendering policy, within the health sector as elsewhere, needs to be conducted in different ways and at different levels.

CONCLUSION

The potentials and gains outlined above might seem minimal, when measured against the endowment of past policy and the forfeit of the equity objectives contained in the Alma Ata declaration. Moreover, a world characterised by increasing political conflict and insecurity, economic belt-tightening and the vulnerability of social policy at a global level, as documented by this book, holds few signposts for progress in the development of effective, equitable and gender-sensitive healthcare. However, we are all too willing to forget or down-play the awareness-raising achievements that have been made by women working in the development field; the growing recognition of the effectiveness of a gender approach to development practice; and the potential for mainstreaming a gender approach offered by the shift towards a socioeconomic perspective in policy.

The health sector has a comparative advantage in that there is already a strong recognition of the health needs of women on the basis of their sex, that is, those needs which derive from their biological role. However, there has been less progress either in terms of analysis or response, in recognising the different health rights and needs of women and men on the basis of gender, that is, those rights and needs which derive from their social roles and relationships in the work place, the place of residence, in cities and the countryside.

It is not sufficient just to recognise the different roles, responsibilities and requirements of women and men in sexual and reproductive health, or even just family health. It is also necessary to recognise the *gender* dimensions of *all* aspects of health and healthcare such as public and environmental health, or the different risks faced by women and men workers in gender-segmented labour markets and different interstices of the informal economy. This is essential in order to understand the biomedical and social synergies between the health of children and their parents at different stages of their life-cycle and to respond to the health rights and needs of all, in sickness and in health.

NOTES

A shorter version of this chapter appeared as 'In Sickness and in Health: Engendering Health Policy for Development' in *Third World Planning Review* 17 (2), 1995. I am grateful for comments on this chapter by Erik Nordberg and Kyllike Christenssen of IHCST, Karolinska Institutet, Stockholm; to Solveig Freudenthal of the Development Study Unit, University of Stockholm; and to Malcolm Alexander of the Southwark Community Health Council, London.

1 While 'sex' refers to biological difference, 'gender' refers to the social relations between women and men. A gender perspective, therefore, is one which recognises socially constructed gender roles and gender relations. These are not universal but context specific.

REFERENCES

Asian & Pacific Women's Resource & Action Series (1990), *Health*, Kuala Lumpur: Asian and Pacific Development Centre.

Basu, A. M. and Basu, K. (1991) 'Women's Economic Roles and Child Survival: The Case of India', *Health Transition Review*, vol. 1, no. 1, April.

Beall, J. (1995) 'In Sickness and in Health: Engendering Health Policy for Development', *Third World Planning Review*, vol. 17, no. 2, May.

Beall, J., Hassim, S. and Todes, A. (1989), '"A Bit on the Side"?: Gender Struggles in the Politics of Transformation in South Africa', *Feminist Review*, no. 33, Autumn.

Beall, J., Kanji, N., Faruqi, F., Hussain, C. M. and Mirani, M. (1994) *Social Safety Nets and Social Networks: Their Role in Poverty Alleviation in Pakistan*. Report to the Overseas Development Administration, London for the World Bank Poverty Assessment for Pakistan.

Bloom, G. H. (1991) 'Managing Health Sector Development: Markets and Institutional Reform', in C. Colclough and J. Manor (eds) *States or Markets? Neo-Liberalism and the Development Policy Debate*, Oxford: Clarendon Press.

Elson, D. (1989) 'The Impact of Structural Adjustment on Women: Concepts and Issues', in B. Onimode (ed.) *The IMF, The World Bank and the African Debt, Volume 2: The Social and Political Impact*, London: Zed Books.

Forsberg, B. C., Musambo, M., Soeters, R., Mulambwa, V. and Joy, D. (1993) 'Health Expenditures and Attitudes to User Fees in a Sub-Saharan Setting', mimeo.

Genberg, H. (1992) 'Macroeconomic Adjustment and the Health Sector: A Review'. Paper presented at the International Conference on Macroeconomics and Health in Countries of Greatest Need, Geneva, 24–26 June.

Hardiman, M. and Midgley, J. (1982) *The Social Dimensions of Development: Social Policy and Planning in the Third World*, New York: John Wiley & Sons.

Harriss, J. (1989) 'Urban Poverty and Urban Poverty Alleviation', *Cities*, August.

Johan, R. (1992) 'Mainstreaming Women in Development in Different Settings'. Paper presented at a seminar on Mainstreaming Women in Development organised by the OECD/DAC/WID Expert Group, Paris, 19–20 May.

Kabeer, N. (1991) 'Gender Production and Well-Being: Rethinking the Household Economy', IDS Discussion Paper 288, Institute of Development Studies, University of Sussex.

—— (1992a) 'From Fertility Reduction to Reproductive Choice: Gender Perspectives on Family Planning', IDS Discussion Paper 299, Institute of Development Studies, University of Sussex.

—— (1992b) 'Evaluating Cost-Benefit Analysis as a Tool for Gender Planning', *Development and Change*, vol. 23, pp. 323–347.

Kabeer, N. and Raikes, A. (eds) (1992) 'Gender and Primary Health Care: Some Forward Looking Strategies', *IDS Bulletin*, vol. 23, no. 1, January.

Levy, C. (1991) 'Critical Issues in Translating Gender Concerns into Planning Competence in the 1990s'. Paper presented at the Joint ACSP and AESOP International Congress, Planning TransAtlantic: Global Change and Local Problems, Oxford, UK, 8–12 July.

—— (1992) 'Gender and the Environment: The Challenge of Cross-Cutting Issues in Development Policy and Planning', *Environment and Urbanization*, vol. 4, no. 1, April.

Lewis, M. A. and Parker, C. (1991) 'Policy and Implementation of User Fees in Jamaican Public Hospitals', *Health Policy*, no. 18.

Molyneux, M. (1985) 'Mobilization Without Emancipation? Women's Interests, State and Revolution in Nicaragua', *Feminist Studies*, vol. 11, no. 2.

Moser, C. (1989) 'Gender Planning in the Third World: Meeting Practical and Strategic Gender Needs', *World Development*, vol. 17, no. 11.

—— (1991) 'From Marginality to Vulnerability: The Changing Agenda of Social Policy from Residual Welfare to Compensatory Measures'. Paper presented at the IDS 25th Anniversary Conference, 6–9 November.

Nazzari, M. (1983) 'The "Woman Question" in Cuba: An Analysis of Material Constraints on its Solution', *Signs*, vol. 9, no. 2.

Nordberg, E. (1993) Personal communication, International Centre for Health Research, Karolinska Institute, Stockholm.

OECD (1995) *Women in the City: Housing, Environment and Urban Services*, Paris: Organisation for Economic Cooperation and Development.

Orubuloye, I. O., Caldwell, J. C., Caldwell, P. and Bledsoe, C. H. (1991) 'The Impact of Family and Budget Structure on Health Treatment in Nigeria', *Health Transition Review*, vol. 1, no. 2, October.

Ostergaard, L. (1992) 'Module 3: Gender and Health', *Gender and Third World Development*, Brighton: Institute of Development Studies, University of Sussex.

Phillips, D. R. (1990) *Health and Health Care in the Third World*, Harlow: Longman.

Pinstrup-Anderson, P. (1992) 'Macroeconomic Adjustment and its Impact on Poor Countries'. Paper presented at the International Conference on Macroeconomics and Health in Countries of Greatest Need, Geneva, 24–26 June.

Raikes, A. (1992) 'Gender and the Production of Health Care Services: Issues for Women's Roles in Health Development', *IDS Bulletin*, vol. 23, no. 1, January.

Sen, G. and Grown, C. (1988) *Development, Crises and Alternative Visions*, London: Earthscan.

Smyke, P. (1991) *Women and Health*, London: Zed Books.

Toye, J. (1987) *Dilemmas of Development*, Oxford: Basil Blackwell.

Welbourn, A. (1991) 'The Social and Economic Dimensions of Poverty and Ill-Health: Based on Fieldwork in Sierra Leone, Uganda and Ghana', mimeo.

—— (1992) 'Rapid Rural Appraisal, Gender and Health – Alternative Ways of Listening to Needs', *IDS Bulletin*, vol. 23, no. 1, January.

Whitehead, A. (1979) 'Some Preliminary Notes on the Subordination of Women', *IDS Bulletin*, vol. 10, no. 3.

WHO (1992a) *Women's Health: Across Age and Frontier*, Geneva: World Health Organisation.

—— (1992b) *Health Dimensions of Economic Reform*, Geneva: World Health Organisation.

WHO/UNICEF (1978) 'Primary Health Care'. Report of the International Conference on Primary Health Care, Alma Ata, USSR.

World Bank (1987) *Financing Health Services in Developing Countries: An*

Agenda for Reform, World Bank Policy Study, Washington, DC: World Bank.

—— (1990) *World Development Report 1990*, New York: Oxford University Press.

Wuyts, M., Mackintosh, M. and Hewitt, T. (1992) *Development Policy and Public Action*, Oxford: Oxford University Press in association with the Open University.

Young, K. et al. (eds) (1981) *Of Marriage and the Market*, London: CSE Books.

6

HOW CAN HUNGARIAN WOMEN LOSE WHAT THEY HAVE NEVER HAD?

Maria Adamik

THE CHANGING SITUATION OF SOCIAL SECURITY IN HUNGARY

According to Zsuzsa Ferge, the social security system of the former state-socialist countries in Eastern Europe did not differ fundamentally from that of capitalist economies (Ferge, 1991: 69–91). Considering both the level of social security costs in terms of GNP and the number of social security programmes, the systems do seem to be similar at first sight.

But this statement does not hold true when one goes into these programmes in more detail. Besides the characteristic absence of unemployment benefits, universal programmes (which remained in place in Hungary until 1990!) and programmes for the automatic indexing of wages, the entire social and societal context of social security programmes was very different in Hungary to those in Western Europe and in Scandinavia.[1] Thus, the new trends introduced during the current transition exhibit both certain traits of the previous social context and characteristics belonging to the market economy of a new-born democracy.

The welfare state is very often conceptualised in exclusively quantitative terms as measured by expenditure, with the assumption being that the greater the expenditure the higher the degree of equality. However, this approach tends to 'neglect qualitative variations in effects of state provision over time and across nations' (Orloff, 1992).

Starting from the possibility of qualitative variations, national differences and gender differences in the impact of welfare state policies can be analysed. It is then also possible to trace the specific impact of the policies belonging to the new democracies, and decide

96

to what extent they can be characterised as new types of welfare states.[2]

Two programmes from Hungary illustrate this sort of situation. The first programme is concerned to counteract weakening social security caused by rising unemployment and by the transition from a system of general social security to a system of individual social insurance, through the introduction of a new system of social assistance.

In the new system, only certain people are eligible to receive benefits. The World Bank has suggested that individual norms should be set for such eligibility, and that clients should be given the right to appeal against decisions of the social administration.[3]

The people formulating the new Social Act have only partially accepted this advice. They have accepted the idea of criteria; in fact, eligibility criteria for receiving social assistance are very strict. An income test has been introduced which measures family income rather than personal income (in contradiction to the logic of a personal income tax system), which applies a new artificial definition of family membership and of members' financial responsibilities towards each other. The test states that family income per capita must be considerably below the officially recognised poverty line in order for someone from the family to be eligible. The level of welfare benefits is then tied to the minimum old age pension, which in itself is approximately half of the current minimum standard of living.[4]

Under this programme, people have no right to appeal against decisions by the local social administration, with the exception of one type of assistance – childcare support. This leaves ample room for the discretionary powers of local social administrations.

The second programme of the new democracy concerns women's issues. The government quickly appointed an EU observer for women's affairs. However, the Hungarian government relied on the Women's Association for this representation. This organisation was previously connected to the communist government.

This alliance between the government and the Women's Association might block the growth of the fledgeling grassroots women's movement, while at the same time managing to satisfy EU expectations with regard to attention for women's issues before joining the EU.[5] It is important to note that during the abortion debate, the Hungarian parliament offered ten times more money to pro-life groups than to the only active grassroots feminist group when it distributed money among NGOs.

Some important conclusions about the previously existing labour market situation and social policy are as follows:

1 The previously existing social provisions were not social rights in the sense used by Marshall. Instead, they could be considered social guarantees, preserving the legitimacy of the socialist system.

2 As both the planned economy and social policy were subordinated to the political system, neither of them could fulfil their primary goal, needed for modernisation; namely, to overcome the mass poverty existing after the Second World War. Such an effort could have occurred, as it did in West European societies in the postwar period. One might say that if the process had included social rights and had been aimed at the private sphere rather than the public, the current transition to democracy could have been less painful and would be more widely supported by women.

3 There was no personal income tax system (until 1988–1989); although wages were set artificially low, certain products and services were heavily subsidised.

4 There was no separate, independent social security budget. The Department still has more form than substance and has no autonomy of its own. As a result, this long-lasting 'temporary' situation gives the government certain room to manoeuvre in handling its huge financial deficit. The range of social benefits was widened according to political priorities, while the source of contributions was not taken into account.

5 When benefits were given according to the principle of full-time employment and the desirable pattern was families with two breadwinners, eligibility criteria in social assistance were not applied (it is an element of the new Social Act). The majority of the benefits were wage-related and directly connected to employment, i.e. to the main employer, the state.

6 The system did not recognise the increasing problems for women, stemming from the hardship of full employment in combination with household duties, and the spread of single-parent families.[6] The use of the word 'poverty' was forbidden (up to the mid-1980s) and personal existential insecurity was not recognised.

7 The educational level of women grew continuously higher, and the rate of employment for women aged 15–54 reached 80 per cent by 1980 (Adamik, 1991a). At a certain stage, Hungarian society with its basically unchanged patriarchal gender roles, apparently made several attempts to re-evaluate the 'socialist way of women's

emancipation', which actually had no historical antecedents.[7] The consequences of such an emancipation could be deemed problematic due to the lack of emancipatory processes in the private sphere. The relatively generous childcare benefits (childcare grant, childcare allowance, i.e. paid, job-protected maternity leave, sick-pay for mothers in case of children's illness) and the availability of child day-care institutions,[8] were interpreted as women's privilege, or at least programmes benefiting mothers.

Divorce has been viewed as deviant behaviour, rather than as the only possibility for individual women to 'practise human rights' or to retain some remnant of human dignity in a traditionally male-dominated culture of an anti-democratic society.

The declining birthrate, increasing divorce rate, growing out-of-wedlock fertility and high abortion rates were seen neither as part of a European trend, nor as problematic signs of gender relations. Both social science and the public suggested that the source of these demographic phenomena must be looked for in the inadequate implementation of women's double roles.

IMPACT OF CURRENT CHANGES IN SOCIAL POLICY

Hungary stood at the beginning of the transition with a governing coalition of centre-right Christian parties. Irrespective of the ruling coalition, there is a general interest within the new and freely elected parliament – which has 93 per cent male MPs[9] – to eliminate every aspect of the 'socialist heritage'. This includes eliminating the previous encouragement of women's employment, reducing childcare benefits both in cash and in kind, and also reducing social services for the elderly. Reducing provisions for children is not in the strict ideological interest of a conservative government – since it worries about the nation's survival. But in practice, the Social Security Fund is no longer willing to finance them (as they are benefits to which people do not contribute first), and it provides an opportunity for the government to reduce its deficit (or at least not to increase it more than is permitted by the World Bank).

The decrease in women's employment goes against the interests of the whole population, as is illustrated by some simple figures. Some 22.6 per cent of the population over sixteen have incomes below the poverty line, together with one-third of all children; altogether, 27 per

ARIA ADAMIK

cent of the population. Another 15 per cent of the population have
incomes around the level of the minimum standard of living. This
means that, regardless of political intentions or re-emerging ideas of
women's traditional roles, families simply cannot afford to depend on
one salary alone. The evidence indicating the importance of employment can be illustrated by the following figures: 45 per cent of
unemployed people, 39 per cent of mothers on childcare leave, and 17
per cent of all pensioners have incomes below the poverty line.

Nevertheless, the income provided by social security benefits
remains limited. Figures demonstrate this as well: 20 per cent of
active earners also fall below the poverty line. By the end of 1992,
families with one child (36 per cent of whom have incomes below the
poverty line) and with two children (the corresponding figure is 33 per
cent) were in a more difficult financial situation than they were a year
before. Some 30 per cent of single-parent families have incomes below
the poverty line, while 41 per cent of Gypsy households belong to the
10 per cent of the population with the lowest incomes.[10]

Legislation concerning social policy mentioned above has been
implemented. Through a process of so-called 'profile-cleaning', the
social security legislation has been altered from a generalised system to
one based on the principle of individual insurance. The Social Security
Fund has been divided into pension and healthcare funds. Financing
family allowances – which had become universal by 1990 – was taken
over by the central budget (i.e. out of taxes). Childcare grants and
childcare allowances were financed by the Social Security Fund up to
1993, while the contribution rate of both employers and employees
remained at the same level (respectively, 43 per cent and 10 per cent of
wages). Moreover, it was increased by establishing a separate Unemployment Fund (respectively, 2 and 1 per cent).

The funds are struggling with huge deficits. Employers are either
reluctant to pay high contributions (thus often use 'black employment') or they simply cannot do so. One of the 'side effects' of rapidly
growing unemployment is, again, shrinking contributions to the
funds. Privatisation has not yet been beneficial for the funds. There
seems to be no solution and the situation is chaotic and fairly
dramatic.[11]

The funds' administration will also have a controlling function
similar to that of the tax authority. The control and punishment of
unemployed people who take 'odd jobs' are to become stricter.
Legislation has shortened the duration of benefits (sick leave, unemployment), restricted their coverage and decreased entitlement to

00

services under social insurance. Nor is there straightforward information available, with the result that no one knows what they are entitled to.

From the government's perspective, the only solution to these problems is to enable full-time motherhood for women, thereby mitigating unemployment and cutting the funds' expenses. Since the cost of full-time motherhood is to be covered by the government, women have to fulfil a certain qualifying period spent in the labour market, i.e. they have to have contributed to the Social Insurance Fund.[12] Contrary to the childcare grant and allowance which could, at least theoretically, be claimed by fathers, the new childcare support can be claimed only by mothers.

A second part of the solution is the introduction of a nursing allowance in the case of women taking care of relatives at home. Mothers who provide care for their relatives, are entitled to crèches, kindergartens and after-school programmes only if they have more than three children. The level of benefits ranges from one-third to a half of the minimum living standard. From these sums, contributions have to be paid to the Social Insurance Funds.

The Social Act seemed to be fairly generous to these full-time 'homemaker women' by promising to add the years spent at home to their qualifying period. However, nothing is irreversible. The Social Act came into force at the beginning of 1993 and this 'generosity' has already been questioned.

The third part of the solution is again very controversial, as it is a step which could have been taken earlier, or later, with fewer effects, but which is currently having very adverse ones. It includes postponing the retirement age of women from fifty-five to sixty,[13] which is proposed for 1995; the qualifying period for a pension has already been extended from ten to twenty years. Thousands of women have suddenly lost their entitlement to an old-age pension, having spent years rearing children, and have now become totally dependent on their families.

Among other planned solutions[14] the following ideas are being mooted. Family allowances will become taxable, and the tax revenue will be channelled into the expenditure for assistance concerning children (childcare support). As for social insurance, part-time pensions will be abolished, the conditions of disability pensions will be made more rigorous,[15] and periods spent in higher education, childcare leave and sick leave will no longer be taken into account when determining the qualifying period for pensions.

Parents were entitled to take sick leave in the case of illness of children up to ten years of age. Putting the cost of sick leave increasingly on the employer will expand the extent to which children's needs are not met and/or multiply the disadvantages of women in the labour market.[16]

Apart from the fact that the Hungarian private sector employs twice as many men as women, there is no reliable information on the attitudes of the growing number of private firms and entrepreneurs towards women employees. There are signs in newspapers of women's defencelessness, although the articles seldom discuss labour contracts as disadvantageous for women or sexual harassment at the work place (although the latter is not an entirely new phenomenon).

Since neither the Hungarian constitution nor the ratification of UN agreements on non-discrimination policies (1982) had any impact on sexual culture – according to which women are objects – how can this very new and still very eager capitalism afford not to use every possible source of dominance, including modern forms of sexism, which exist in harmony with traditional patterns?

In addition, there are growing commercial interests, both domestic and foreign, which employ young women for various commercial sexual activities. Public scandal erupted only when newly born children were used as objects of trade.

Unemployment in general terms is a severe (and to the Hungarians a shocking) result of the transition. It is obviously not to be simply understood in terms of its impact in lowering economic security, even though that is a basic consideration. One also has to consider its consequences on people's mental health. Although women still numerically represent a smaller proportion of unemployed people than men, the figure is higher among young, less educated women.[17] The rigidity of the school system and the increasing size of the cohort entering the labour market in the next few years will make this female population even more vulnerable than their mothers were.

Social integration has weakened further: the life strategy of the mothers' generation is largely irrelevant for the daughters' generation, and the already existing gap between women in different social strata will widen. Both these psychological and social phenomena make it difficult for women to recognise their common interests and to develop solidarity. While state social provisions, even if already established, can be reversed, the aforementioned psychological and social trends are probably irreversible.

The prevailing discussion in circles concerned with social development is how to overcome economic constraints and help needy people in order to make the introduction of the market economy possible. No attention is paid to the fact that through its social policy the state actually regulates gender relations. Neither political forces nor civic movements undertake to interpret women's issues as a cornerstone of democracy in Hungary.

The differences in the various approaches that emerged in the EU concerning the interpretation of democracy along with unification, and issues such as emigration, etc., make it difficult to incorporate the lessons learned from a long tradition of Western women's movements in shaping democracy in Hungary.

From a Central European point of view the only remedy for creating a women-friendly, user-friendly[18] society is to consider Peter Flora's suggestion concerning the future of welfare states. A hundred years of development of European welfare states is based on the economic surplus produced in the market economy. If growth should no longer provide the basis of a welfare state, Flora's three new consensuses could replace it: a new consensus between the state and its citizens, between generations, and a new consensus between genders.[19]

Needless to say, there is no real probability of changing the prevailing way of thinking. While the new European issue is 'Can the welfare state compete?',[20] the regional costs of competing to 'join Europe' will be paid overwhelmingly – in addition to certain social strata – by women.

NOTES

1 I distinguish three different scenarios in Europe according to the historical development of women's situation and the main features of welfare states. Scenario 1 belongs to Scandinavian history, Scenario 2 to West Europe (EU) and Scenario 3 is the particular development of women's situation shaped by state-socialism. For more details see Adamik (1992).

2 By the term 'welfare state' I mean rather the *goal* declared by these Central European democracies rather than their *actual achievement*. Moreover, one might be generally sceptical like A. S. Orloff (1992), according to whom

> one should use the term 'state social provision' rather than the 'welfare state' to avoid assuming what must in fact be proved: that states promote the welfare of their citizens through the mechanism of social policy, as well as to avoid assuming that such a commitment, once established, is irreversible – an assumption

whose untenability must be especially clear to readers in the United States and United Kingdom.

(Orloff, 1992)

3 See Kessides et al. (1991–1992).

4 Figures for 1993 showed that the old-age pension amounted to 6,300 Ft (one British pound being equal to 120 Ft). The minimum wage was 9,000 Ft as agreed by employers and trade unions – even though the ruling was not enforced. At the same time, the minimum cost of living stood at 12,000 Ft per capita because of the imposition of VAT.

5 The very first Women's Studies Center was established with government support at the Budapest University of Economics, which traditionally had strong connections with the Women's Association. While, on the one hand, the existence of the Center is good news, on the other hand, the director publicly refuses to apply 'feminist' approaches. This may suggest that Hungarian Social Science is still not ready to alter its previous attitude toward women, according to which women are mothers, wives and a flexible labour force. Therefore, the first Women's Studies Center is likely to underwrite recent government policy with its consequent impact on women.

6 Before the transition, the situation of single mothers led neither to major dependency – there was no considerable benefit – nor to poverty, as they were generally employed (unlike the effect of the programme of the Aid to Families with Dependent Children (AFDC) in the USA). Recently, their situation has been worsening. The very first step of the transition was to abolish subsidies on children's clothing, then on basic food items like milk and bread. The cost of maintaining an apartment (rent, interest rate on loans, energy costs) has also increased.

7 This statement is obviously a crude one. There was a Feminist Association at the beginning of this century when a radical–liberal wing existed in the Hungarian social movement for a short period. The women of an overwhelmingly underdeveloped agricultural society couldn't join the high/middle-class feminist movement. To put it another way, the middle class itself was too weak. The social democratic women's movement could have provided women with a great tradition if both the party and its women's movement hadn't been channelled into the Communist Party and its women's 'movement' in 1948.

8 See Adamik (1991a) for a description of the entire parenting policy.

9 For more details about women and the 1990 parliamentary elections in Hungary, see Adamik (1991b) and Fodor (1992).

10 Survey on Households, TÁRKI, Dec. 1992, pp. 18–19.

11 Pensioners have organised themselves and have become a partner in negotiations at governmental level. After the introduction of insurance cards – in order to measure the achievement of general practitioners – the reform of the health system came to a sudden stop. Besides administrative difficulties and chaos there is little real change. The lack of money constantly produces a situation which causes direct danger to clients' lives.

12 Thus, the majority of Gypsy women are excluded. While an Act for Minorities is to be proposed and the leaders of different Gypsy groups are negotiating with the government, no one recognises – including the male group leaders – how sexism is interlinked with racism.

13 In comparison with other countries, fifty-five is very low; and it is lower than the retirement age for men (sixty). These are two arguments in favour of altering the arrangement. A counter-argument is that such low retirement ages are justified by the life expectancy of both sexes, which is about six to eight years below the European average.

14 'Szigorítások minden területen' ('Tightening up in every field'), *Magyar Hirlap*, 19 March 1993, p. 11.

15 At the beginning of the 1990s, more than one-third (40 per cent) of new pensioners had a right to a pension due to disability.

16 Under the reform of social security the cost of the first ten days has already been transferred to employers. According to a new proposal, they should pay the first thirty days.

17 The structure of the Hungarian school system is essential for understanding this phenomenon. For more details see Adamik, Ladó and Tóth (1991).

18 Phrases cited from Maria Helga Hernes (1989) and Laura Balbo (1987).

19 Peter Flora (1986).

20 Pfaller, Gough and Thernborn (1991).

REFERENCES

Adamik, M. (1991a) 'Supporting Parenting and Child Rearing', in S. Kamerman and A. Kahn *Child Care, Parental Leave and the under 3s*, New York: Auburn House.

—— (1991b) 'A Loss of Rights', *Feminist Review*, Autumn.

—— (1992) *Where Still Nothing has Changed*, unpublished manuscript, Budapest.

—— (1993) 'Feminism and Hungary', in N. Funk and M. Mueller (eds) *Gender Politics and Post-Communism*, New York: Routledge.

Adamik, M., Ladó, M. and Tóth, F. (1991) *Training for Women under Condition of Crisis and Structural Adjustment*, manuscript prepared for the ILO.

Balbo, L. (1987) *Time to Care*, Milan: F. Angeli.

Corrin, C. (1993) *Magyar Women: Hungarian Women's Lives 1960s–1990s*, Basingstoke: Macmillan.

Ferge, Zs. (1991) 'Social Security Systems in the New Democracies of Central and Eastern Europe: Past Legacies and Possible Futures', in G. A. Cornia and S. Sipos (eds) *Children and the Transition to the Market Economy: A Study by UNICEF*, Avebury: Aldershot.

—— (1992) *Modernization, the Breakdown of Social Integration and the Case of Children*, manuscript prepared for UNICEF, Paris.

Flora, P. (1986) *Growth to Limits: The Welfare States since World War II*, Berlin: W. D. Gruyter.

Flora, P. and Heidenheimer, A. (1981) 'The Historical Core and Changing

Boundaries of the Welfare States', in P. Flora and A. Heidenheimer (eds) *The Development of Welfare States in Europe and America*, New Brunswick, NJ: Transaction Books.

Fodor, É. (1992) *The Gender Gap in the Hungarian Elections of 1990*, UCLA, Department of Sociology, Los Angeles, unpublished manuscript.

Goven, J. (1993) 'Gender Politics in Hungary: Autonomy and Antifeminism', in N. Funk and M. Mueller (eds) *Gender Politics and Post-Communism*, New York: Routledge.

Heller, M., Némedi, D. and Rényi, Å. (1990) *Népesedési viták 1963–1986 (Debates on Population Policy 1963–1986)*, vol. 2, Budapest: Századvég.

Hernes, M. H. (1989) *Welfare State and Women Power*, Oslo: Norwegian University Press.

Hobson, B. (1990) 'No Exit, No Voice: Women's Economic Dependency and the Welfare State', *Acta Sociologica*, vol. 33.

Kessides et al. (1991–1992), *Szociálpoltika és elosztási rendszer (Social Policy and System of Distribution)*, Shortened Report for the World Bank: Esély.

Offe, C. (1984) *The Contradiction of the Welfare State*, Cambridge: MIT Press.

Orloff, A. S. (1992) *Gender and the Social Rights of Citizenship*. Paper presented at the Conference on Poverty, Social Welfare and Social Policy, Bremen, 3–6 September.

Pfaller, A., Gough, I. and Thernborn, G. (eds) (1991) *Can the Welfare State Compete?*, London: Macmillan.

Szalai, J. (1991) 'Some Aspects of the Changing Situation of Women in Hungary', *Signs*, vol. 17, no. 1, Autumn.

7

ECONOMIC RESTRUCTURING IN MALAYSIA

Implications for Women Workers

Chee Heng Leng and Cecilia Ng Choon Sim

INTRODUCTION

Malaysia, one of the recent Newly Industrialising Countries (NICs), is often touted as an economic success story. With high growth rates and significant capital accumulation, built on the basis of free trade and a pro-capitalist open economy, it is held by the World Bank and the International Monetary Fund (IMF) to be a role model for other Third World countries. None the less, the country felt the full impact of the world economic recession in the 1980s, which eventually forced the government to undertake various 'economic restructuring' measures. By the late 1980s, however, the economy seemed to have recovered its high growth rates. Now, the country is once again considered exemplary, having weathered successfully the global economic crisis with structural adjustments not unlike those recommended by the World Bank and the IMF.[1]

In order to address the central questions posed by the Introduction to this volume, concerning the impact of global changes on women and their responses, in this chapter we shall examine the costs of Malaysia's economic success, particularly for women workers. Although economic growth has resulted in higher incomes and standards of living for the population in general, and greater employment opportunities for women workers in particular, the quality of this employment is called into question. The virtually free hand that has been given to investors and management has led to work intensification, work fragmentation, and practices such as labour flexibilisation, all of which have detrimental effects on the welfare, security and health of women workers. Furthermore, particular work organisation methods and human resource management tactics erode worker unity and increase their vulnerability. Malaysia's success as a foreign investment centre has also been at the expense of workers' rights.

This chapter is organised in five sections. After this introduction, we give a brief description of the Malaysian economy and the structural adjustment which took place in the mid-1980s, and suggest several reasons for its success. Following this is a discussion of the various effects this economic restructuring has had on women workers. We then examine the implications with regard to workers' rights and the nature of their responses, before summarising our arguments in the concluding section.

To support our arguments, we draw upon recent secondary sources as well as primary data from our own research: a 1990–1992 study of women office workers in four large companies which apply information technology, and a much smaller set of interviews with women electronics workers carried out in 1992.[2]

GROWTH AND STRUCTURAL ADJUSTMENT IN THE MALAYSIAN ECONOMY

Since British colonial days, the Malaysian economy has thrived on the production of primary commodities for export. A leading producer and exporter of tin and rubber at the time of Independence (1957), Malaysia also became a chief producer and exporter of palm oil and tropical hardwoods in the 1960s. From the mid-1970s, petroleum became increasingly important.

The success of the Malaysian economy owes much to the favourable economic environment created by the postwar economic boom which lasted until the 1960s.[3] Although there was a nose-dive in primary commodity prices in the early 1970s, the late 1970s boom in world trade particularly benefited Malaysia. In fact, this is considered Malaysia's major post-Independence commodity export boom, when commodity exports more than trebled in five years, from M$9.2bn in 1975 to M$28.2bn in 1980 (Jomo, 1990: 59).

Industrialisation also played a major role in the success of the Malaysian economy. In the early 1970s, the Malaysian government switched its industrial strategy from import substitution to export orientation,[4] and waged an aggressive campaign to woo foreign investors. This coincided with a turning point in the economies of the industrialised nations: there, in the 1960s, rising wages, increasing competitiveness and difficulty in controlling labour led to the relocation of direct investment to Third World sites.[5]

Although Malaysian wage rates were not the lowest in the region, it had other important attractions such as political stability, and good infrastructure. More significantly, the government bent over backwards to encourage foreign investment by creating Free Trade Zones with infrastructures in place, offering lucrative tax breaks, maintaining a low wage policy and controlling labour (Rajah, 1992).

Economic recession

In the early 1980s, however, the prices of Malaysia's primary export commodities – rubber, tin, palm oil, petroleum – fell. The industrial sector was also badly affected by the world recession. But even though there was decreased world trade, recession and a deterioration of terms of trade in the early 1980s, the Malaysian government expected the adverse commodity price movements to be temporary and responded to the world economic crisis with increased spending (Demery and Demery, 1992).[6]

The years from 1979 to 1984 were therefore a period of economic expansion, high growth rates and high rates of domestic price inflation. There was a surge in government expenditure, especially development expenditure, particularly in 1981–1982, leading to a growing overall deficit – 8 per cent of GDP in 1979, 21.7 per cent in 1981, and 18.9 per cent in 1982 – which had to be financed by foreign borrowing (ibid.: 37).[7] This growth was not sustainable in the long run because of the increasing deficit, increasing debt and continued deterioration in the terms of trade. In fact, it made the Malaysian economy even more vulnerable to external pressures. Finally, in 1985–1986, the government decided to reduce foreign borrowing and cut back public expenditure, which resulted in severe recession (Jomo, 1990: 52).

Employment of workers suffered most during the recession years of the mid-1980s. Between 1983 and 1987, 96,000 workers were fired, 50,568 of whom had been employed in the manufacturing sector[8] (*Star*, 2 July 1987, cited in Johan et al.,1992). Unemployment shot up from less than 5 per cent to 6.9 per cent in 1985, and then to 8.2 per cent in 1987; the number of unemployed workers more than doubled between 1982 and 1986, crossing the half-million mark.

Structural adjustment

Malaysia's foreign borrowing never reached the level where it had to be subjected to IMF stabilisation policies and World Bank structural adjustment programmes. Nevertheless, after the 1985–1986 recession, there was a clear governmental emphasis on 'structural adjustment' and 'deregulation' (actualised in practice as privatisation), a liberalised export-oriented environment and attempts towards 'labour flexibilisation' (Johan et al., 1992: 26). Thus, although the Malaysian state is able to determine its own priorities to a certain extent, its economic restructuring has components similar to the structural adjustment programmes advocated by the World Bank and the IMF (Jayaweera, 1993).

Essentially, the strategy aims at cutting public expenditure, strengthening the balance of payments and encouraging the private sector to play a greater role in the economy. Toward these ends, there was a large reduction in government development expenditure, and the privatisation of government enterprises, especially public services such as the National Electricity Board and the Telecom Department. There was also a shift toward relying more on domestic loans to finance public expenditure, and in order to improve the balance of payments exports were encouraged by the revision of export duties, liberalisation of the Export Credit Refinancing Scheme and exemption from duty for indirect exporters.

Foreign investment was encouraged by further liberalisation of the 1975 Industrial Coordination Act in 1985, amendments to the Promotion of Investment Act 1986 and relaxation of the policy on foreign equity as well as the requirements for manufacturing licences.[9] In the services sector, there was promotion of tourism and the setting up of programmes to twin educational colleges, which respectively helped to earn foreign exchange and keep it within the country (HAWA, 1993).

The Industrial Master Plan[10] published in early 1986 stressed the importance that would be accorded to export-oriented industry. This document analyses the problems in the industrial sector, chief among which is a high level of technological dependence and lopsidedness.[11] The emphasis, therefore, is on the development of export-oriented, high-value-added, high-technology industries. The emphasis on technological upgrading and export market orientation is reiterated in the Sixth Malaysia Plan (1991–1995) (Malaysia, 1991: 137–139). In the future, industrial development will emphasise greater automation and other labour-saving production processes to reduce labour utilisation. In this respect, information technology has also been identified as a key technology which is needed to support the transformation of Malaysian society into a high-tech industrial society (Malaysia, 1989: 177).

Economic recovery

From a negative GDP growth rate of 1 per cent in 1985, the Malaysian economy had recovered sufficiently by 1987 to register a GDP growth rate of 5.4 per cent. Between 1988 and 1992, GDP grew at an average of about 9 per cent per annum. Likewise, the rate of growth in per capita income was 5.5 per cent in 1985 and 9.6 per cent in 1986; but by 1987, it had become 9 per cent, and from 1988 to 1991 it was 12 per cent, 10.0 per cent, 10 per cent and 9.2 per cent.[12] Furthermore, the exchange rate came down, and inflation seems to have been contained at about 5 per cent.

The success of the Malaysian structural adjustment hinges upon its industrial sector (Jomo, 1990). The growth in the economy after 1987 is due to the growth of industry and related services. Manufacturing has overtaken agriculture to become the largest sector contributing to GDP. In 1985, agriculture and forestry contributed 20.8 per cent of GDP and manufacturing contributed 19.7 per cent. In 1990, agriculture's share dropped to 18.7 per cent while manufacturing's share increased to 27 per cent, and was projected to grow to 32.4 per cent in 1995 (Malaysia, 1991: 20).

In terms of employment, increases were registered between 1985 and 1990 in manufacturing (from 15.2 per cent to 19.5 per cent of the labour force), and non-government services (from 30.5 per cent to 32.9 per cent), while decreases were seen in agriculture and forestry (from 31.3 per cent to 27.8 per cent), mining and quarrying (from 0.85 per cent to 0.6 per cent), construction (from 7.6 per cent to 6.4 per cent) and government services (from 14.6 per cent to 12.8 per cent) (Malaysia, 1991: 28).

This growth has been attributed to the liberalised investment policies, relatively good infrastructure, and labour policies – flexibilisation, repression, allowing immigrant labour – which keep labour costs down (Jomo, 1990: 118–142). All this led to the improved competitiveness of Malaysian manufacturing (Demery and Demery, 1992: 61). Despite the major influx of investment, however, the unemployment rate remained high throughout 1988 (8.1 per cent) and 1989 (7.1 per cent) before slowly dropping to 6.3 per cent in 1990 and 5.6 per cent in 1991 (Demery and Demery, 1992). Wages remained high after 1984 due to the inflexibility of existing wages, but since new wage offers were lower in 1986–1987, the average wage declined due to the increasing weight given to the low wages of new entrants into the labour force. By 1990, the country faced an absolute shortage of labour, especially skilled labour (Johan et al., 1992: 27). Wage rates had gone up; collective agreements concluded in 1989 in the private sector managed to obtain increments averaging 7.3 per cent, higher than the rate of inflation.[13] Presently, Malaysia faces the problems of managing growth, the major concerns being the balance of payments, the threat of inflation, labour shortages and infrastructural bottlenecks such as the current power crisis (HAWA, 1993: 5).[14]

EFFECTS ON WOMEN WORKERS

Being an NIC, Malaysia's experience with structural adjustment has been more positive than those of other Third World countries that underwent the World Bank–IMF programmes. Income levels and poverty incidence, for instance, did not deteriorate markedly even during the difficult period of 1984–1987.[15]

In many of the Third World countries that have implemented World Bank–IMF structural adjustment programmes, women have suffered a disproportionate share of the negative consequences. In terms of employment, large proportions of women in the formal sector have lost their jobs, leading to a greater involvement in informal sector work (Commonwealth Secretariat, 1993). In some Latin American countries, women are forced into the informal sector, doing home-based work and casual labour (Nash, 1988), while in some Asian countries more women become unpaid family helpers (Jayaweera, 1993). Unlike these other Third World countries, however, the female participation rate in the Malaysian labour force increased from 44.3 per cent in 1985 to 47.5 per cent in 1991 (HAWA, 1993). From 1985 to 1990, the proportion of women workers either increased or did not change significantly in every occupational category except for agriculture, where women's participation rate dropped from 33.7 per cent to 28.1 per cent (HAWA, 1993).[16] This pattern is actually part of a longer-term trend which can be traced from 1970. The proportion of women working as unpaid family workers in the traditional and informal sectors fell from 39.7 per cent in 1970 to 21.6 per cent in 1990 as women were increasingly absorbed into the modern sectors, particularly the manufacturing and service sectors. The proportion of women classified as employees rose from 38.9 per cent to 62.9 per cent in the same period (HAWA, 1993).

The proportion of women in the manufacturing industries has increased steadily, although slowing down in the early 1980s (from 8.1 per cent in 1970, to 16.3 per cent in 1980, 18.9 per cent in 1985 and 24.3 per cent in 1990); the proportion of women in the services sector has also increased, from 16.4 per cent in 1970 to 21.4 per cent in 1990. Furthermore, the percentage of female employment relative to male employment has increased from an average of 34.6 per cent in 1985 to 35 per cent in 1990. This percentage increase has come from an increase in every sector except for agriculture and forestry, construction, and finance, insurance, real estate and business services (Malaysia, 1991: 415).

In the public sector, female employment also increased from 29.3 per cent of total employment in 1985 to 32.9 per cent in 1990 (HAWA, 1993: 10). In this respect, women government workers in Malaysia seem to have avoided the fate of their counterparts in the other structural adjustment countries, where cuts in public expenditure have reduced public sector employment opportunities (Elson, 1993).

Gender hierarchy in employment

Although from the perspective of employment Malaysian women workers did not fare as badly as those in other Third World countries undergoing structural adjustment programmes, they do, however, experience many similar effects of increased market orientation such as job intensification, flexibilisation and worsening working conditions.

Women workers in the private sector face a deterioration of employment conditions as there is a tendency for work to be over-intensified, leading to adverse effects for health and safety (Elson, 1993). In the export manufacturing industries, women work longer hours and do more intense work under strict discipline. The high speed, repetitive and monotonous nature of their work leads to many health and safety problems. Their condition is exacerbated by the lack of organising rights. In so far as women workers tend to be concentrated in the lower-end, less skilled and less secure jobs, these situations affect them disproportionately. The majority of women employed in manufacturing are in the lowest hierarchy as production and related workers; the proportion of women in this category having increased from 10.4 per cent of the total number of women employed in 1970, to 17.6 per cent in 1980, 17.7 per cent in 1985 and 22.3 per cent in 1990.

Information technology is one of the fastest growing industries in Malaysia today and computerisation has led to a large increase in the number of computer-related jobs.[17] Among computer workers, the higher paid, more technical occupations (systems analysts) are primarily occupied by men. Middle-level jobs (computer programmers) have slightly more women than men; but low-level jobs – data entry operators, typists and clerks – are overwhelmingly filled by women (Ng and Othman, 1992).

It was also found in TELMAL (telecommunications company), that it is much more difficult for women to be promoted. Of all the women in the study, 64 per cent have been in their jobs for less than ten years, 27 per cent for eleven to twenty years, and 9 per cent for more than twenty-one years. This compares unfavourably with the men respondents, 94 per cent of whom have been in their jobs for less than ten years. The men were promoted after an average of four years, the women after nine and a half years.

Even in the public sector, a large proportion (82.3 per cent) of the women employed can be found in the lower categories – primary school teachers, nurses, office and clerical workers, and unskilled general workers.

Insecurity and flexibilisation

The basic problem for Malaysian workers is employment security (Johan et al., 1992: 26–32). As the 1985–1986 economic crisis has shown, employers fired workers freely because under the labour laws redundancy benefits to workers are minimal and not costly to employers. As Malaysia is not a welfare state, there are no unemployment benefits or social security for workers who are out of a job.

Even security in the case of occupational disablement and disease is inadequate. The Social Security Organisation (SOCSO) set up in 1971 as an insurance scheme for workers' health and safety has only given out compensation for industrial accidents, and very minimally at that (Devaraj, 1989). Moreover, SOCSO membership, compulsory for all employees earning MR2,000 and below, precludes workers from seeking compensation from their employers – including taking legal action for negligence – in the case of industrial accidents and disease. In the period of economic crisis, the rate of permanent disablement in the manufacturing sector increased from 7 per 10,000 workers (1980) to 16.8 (1988) (Khor, 1992).

There is also very little income security for workers as no minimum wage legislation exists; nor is there any indexation of the basic wage to some basic cost of living index. Instead, employers are calling for wage systems which peg wages onto individual productivity and output. In fact, the government has already led the way with its New Remuneration System, whereby, for the first time in history, wages of civil servants are determined by assessment of their performance.

Employers are using various ways to achieve 'labour flexibility', by which they mean numerical and wage flexibility. More workers are employed on a term contract basis and can be terminated when their contract is over. In early 1991, there was a new intake of telephone operators in the international section of TELMAL (telecommunications company) to meet rising customer demand. These new workers, mainly women, were recruited on a contract basis. Similarly, in 1992, in BANKAM (local bank), women contract workers were hired as bank tellers.

The use of discretionary payments to supplement basic pay, in other words, wage flexibility, has already been practised by many electronics firms since the 1970s. For example, workers are paid a basic wage which they need to supplement with shift allowances,[18] overtime allowances and various incentive allowances, including an allowance for non-absenteeism, which includes not taking any sick leave.[19] At least one electronics company is known to achieve numerical flexibility by keeping a leaner workforce than it actually needs. Its workers work two shifts and permanent overtime rather than the usual three shifts. In this system, the time between shifts is filled by workers working overtime.[20]

A few other large multinational electronics companies try to reduce labour costs by having their workers work their three shifts in four rotating crews. Each crew works each shift for six full days followed by two rest days on a rotating basis.[21] In this way, Sunday is considered a normal work day and the company does not have to pay overtime allowances for Sunday work. Wage flexibility is also achieved by rewarding workers on the basis of performance. Increments are based on individual performance, so workers compete with each other to earn more.[22] In this way, labour is fragmented as individuals can compete with each other to perform better and earn more. It has been suggested that this may be one reason why it is difficult for electronics workers to organise themselves.[23]

CHEE HENG LENG AND CECILIA NG CHOON SIM

Work organisation, intensification and surveillance

In the intensely competitive economic situation, higher technology and greater automation have led to changes in work organisation, often for the worse from the perspective of workers' well-being. Work has intensified, and there is closer supervision, stricter discipline, less control by workers over their work process, and a heightened sense of alienation due to increasing separation and fragmentation.

The nature of work on a manufacturing assembly line is intense, tedious and repetitive. With higher technology come demands for higher productivity and higher-quality products. This is achieved by the ever-present pressure on workers to achieve the 'target', a production quota which is continually revised upwards and never downwards.[24] In the electronics industry, the new work organisation requires strict discipline and absolute cleanliness from the workers. This has led to working attire which completely covers up a person, strict control over workers walking around the factory, and absolute punctuality, all of which increase regimentation, tension and restricts communication between the workers.[25]

Office workers face similar work situations. In TELMAL, data-entry operators are required to perform 10,000 to 14,000 keystrokes per hour, and their daily productivity report is posted on the wall for public viewing the following morning. The work of the international telephonists at TELMAL has also intensified with the introduction of a computerised exchange in 1985–1987 and with privatisation. Previously, they had more control over their work process – manually writing down information, collecting the tickets at the end of the day, checking and arranging them by country, and then sending the final accounts to the billing section. Now, they are required to fulfil a quota of 3,000 calls per day, or to complete a call within ten seconds. Their productivity is monitored by computer and they are given a monthly report of their performance (Ng, 1992: 26). As a result of all this, the Executive Director of TELMAL was proud to note in a seminar address in 1991 that the expansion of services, customer base, and substantial increase in profits in 1988–1990 were achieved and managed practically without any increase in the number of employees.

At MANAS (airline company), with computerised hunting lines, calls are automatically distributed to the airline's reservations clerks who are required to complete a call within three minutes. They are given a quota of 150 calls per day to handle. Their calls, as well as the

116

quality of their conversation, are monitored through the supervisory console and information on this is printed out every hour.

Productivity-linked incentive schemes are sometimes used to discover the highest level of productivity possible and thereby to intensify the work process. In PUBS (public sector agency), for example, the data-entry operators, whose quota was 11,000 key-strokes per hour, were offered two hours off work for every four days in which they could key in 15,000 keystrokes. When it was found that this level of work could be accomplished, the incentive scheme was scrapped and the quota increased (Ng, 1992: 25). Like the factory workers, these office workers are generally not allowed to move around freely, nor to speak to their colleagues. They are extremely tense and harassed.[26] Even for clerks with a certain degree of freedom of movement, it is noted that there are now more restrictions with the onset of privatisation.[27]

Skilling, de-skilling, displacement

Often, when a work process is automated, or when the technology of a work process is upgraded, women workers are displaced in favour of men because it is assumed that the women cannot be trained in the new skills. This was observed at an electronics factory[28] in a section where machines are used to place electronics components onto printed circuit boards. Previously, it was done manually by women workers, but with the machines, fewer workers are needed, and male workers are trained to do this job.

Whereas in the 1970s the proportion of women employed in the electronics industry was more than 80 per cent, a 1986 survey shows that it has decreased to 67 per cent. While redundancy exercises primarily affected women line operators, job opportunities created by automation were largely for men (Suresh and Rajah, 1992: 20). For office workers in TELMAL, many routine clerical and technical tasks have been eliminated with the development of an automated system for customer services. With the upgrading towards the digital switch system, several exchanges have been closed and telephone operators made redundant. It is estimated that there has been a reduction of 200 staff members who have been redeployed to other sections while new staff – mainly systems analysts and programmers – have been recruited. De-skilling has taken place in the case of former typists who were redeployed as data-entry operators.

On the other hand, computerisation has been beneficial to certain groups of workers. This is usually the case for small work groups with specific clerical and typing responsibilities. One example in TELMAL is the work group of five women clerks who handle the mobile maritime service, for whom the introduction of two personal computers in 1989 has made the work load lighter and easier, with more control over their work process. The male clerks in MANAS have undergone a similar 'skilling' experience with the introduction of computer terminals in 1987. In general, decentralised control and increased flexibility seem to be possible for specific types of workers.

Occupational health and safety

In the chemical-intensive electronics industry, chemical hazards abound. Chemical fumes cause respiratory and dermatological problems and poorly designed work processes with inadequate ventilation make the situation worse.[29]

The electronics factory mould room is notorious among the workers for its chemical dust. There was a spate of cancer (mostly lung cancer) deaths among the women working in the mould room in a particular factory in 1989. Two women had died while still on the job, while four others had stopped working due to their health problems, and subsequently died in their village homes.[30] Compensation was paid, the public did not know about it and no inquiry was conducted.[31]

In the older work processes, electronics workers still suffer from eye strain and migraines due to working with a microscope, while in the newer technological processes, workers confront hazards from using video display terminals.[32] Office and computer workers using the video display unit (VDU) suffer from repetitive strain injuries, wrist joint pain, stiffness, numbness, eye strain and vision problems, muscle aches, and tingling in the shoulders, necks and back, and migraines. Severe problems associated with the organisation of work – chronic exhaustion, anxiety and stress – are also reported by the workers.

In the PUBS study, ten out of forty-two data-entry operators (24 per cent) have had spontaneous abortions within the last three years. Although the direct relationship between effects of VDU radiation and spontaneous abortions are still unproven, these abortions are obviously related to the stress and tension in the job. Various health problems – eating disorders, gastritis, insomnia – are reported by the shift workers in our studies.[33] The strict discipline and the monotonous, fast-paced work induce a high level of stress. Mass hysteria among electronics women workers was a common occurrence in the 1970s, but seems to be occurring less often now.[34]

EROSION OF WORKERS' RIGHTS
AND WORKERS' RESPONSE

The position of the workers is precarious primarily because of their lack of unionisation. Overall, only 10 per cent of the workforce is unionised, and under 12 per cent of the manufacturing workers is unionised. The Malaysian government inherited a legacy of repression from the British colonialists. Legislation curbing workers' rights – such as the Trade Disputes Ordinance of 1949, which severely curbed workers' right to strike, and the Employment Ordinance of 1955, which allowed employers to dismiss workers even on such grounds as *alleged* misconduct – were instituted from colonial times.

Through the 1960s and 1970s, new legislation as well as amendments to existing legislation further curbed workers' rights. For example, compulsory arbitration legislation in 1965 limited the right to strike in a wide range of 'essential services', which included the pineapple canning industry. Subsequent amendments to the Industrial Relations Act of 1967 even preclude certain issues – such as management prerogatives over dismissals – from negotiation. In the early 1970s, workers' rights were tightened by new legislation further limiting the right to strike, strengthening the power of management and curbing the emergence of new independent unions (Jomo, 1990: 87).

The Malaysian Airline System (MAS) industrial dispute of 1978–1979 marked the beginning of a new era of anti-labour policies in line with the market-oriented development strategy of the 1980s. The MAS industrial action was brought to an end by government intervention which included detaining several active union leaders under the Internal Security Act, a law which provides for indefinite detention without trial. In 1980, following the MAS strike, further amendments were made to existing labour laws, which further restricted union rights and extended government control over them. The 1983 'Look East' policy sought to inculcate company loyalty among workers, and encouraged in-house unions. The effects of all this are a declining proportion of the labour force that is unionised and a declining proportion of work-days lost due to industrial action.

The bargaining position of labour is further weakened by the influx of illegal immigrant labour from neighbouring countries. Recently, the government registered and legalised immigrant labour for a few selected jobs; nevertheless, widespread use of low-cost immigrant labour and contract labour serves to depress real wages.[35]

Response of women workers

The participation of women in trade unions is much lower than that of men. In 1980, when women made up 32.2 per cent of the labour force, they only made up 27.1 per cent of total union membership. Through the 1980s, the gender composition of unions remained at around this level, increasing only slightly to 29.9 per cent in 1988 (Rohana, 1991).

Union leadership is generally dominated by men,[36] who often disregard issues which are relevant to women workers. For example, although the women data-entry operators in PUBS belong to a union, when they were involved in a struggle with management to improve their wage levels to be commensurate with the higher quota of keystrokes to which they were subjected, the union was not involved (Ng, 1992: 25). In TELMAL, when typists, teleprinter typists and various operators were subjected to a speed test, instead of opposing the test, the union demanded the value of four annual increments for them. Likewise, the 1987 collective agreement asked that workers exposed to the emission of microwave or other radiation be paid a hazard allowance, instead of demanding changes in work organisation which would eliminate, or at least minimise, the effects of such radiation (Ng, 1992: 23).

Manufacturing industries in free trade zones that employ large numbers of women have had pioneer status since their establishment in the 1970s. Their workers are not allowed to join unions, although unions are not legally banned. Although much has been written about the docility, obedience and lack of consciousness of these workers, they have time and again brought public attention to bear upon their plight by organising spontaneous strikes.[37] During the labour shortage of 1980, there was a spate of wildcat strikes in the Bayan Lepas Free Trade Zone in Penang to demand higher wages (*New Straits Times*, 25 September 1980).

The 900-odd Ruf workers, the majority of whom were women, laid down their tools on 19 September 1980 to demand an increase in wages in line with a fifty-minute increase in working time as well as the increased cost of living (*Star*, 7 October 1980; *New Straits Times*, 23–27 September 1980). The riot police had to be called in to control them (*Star*, 26 September 1980). Ironically, this protest action was eventually dissolved by the Electrical Industry Workers Union Executive Secretary, Anthony Bosco, who intervened and persuaded the workers to drop their demands (*New Straits Times*, 26 September 1980).

During the height of the economic crisis, on 23 September 1985, about 700 workers, again mainly women, fired by the Mostek Electronics Factory in the Bayan Lepas Free Trade Zone, picketed outside their factory gates to demand reinstatement or rightful compensation. They took their protest to the Labour Office and then to the Chief Minister's Office, where they staged sit-ins, marched and waved banners. Their picketing lasted a full thirty-two days (Lochead, 1987).

More recently, in June 1990, the workers of Hitachi Consumers Electronics in Bangi (on the outskirts of Kuala Lumpur), 80 per cent women, went on strike to demand higher pay, no compulsory overtime and the right to form a union. The struggle by workers at RCA, a large multinational electronics company located in the Ulu Kelang Free Trade Zone, to establish an in-house union began in January 1989 when the government announced that electronics workers are allowed to form in-house unions. Nevertheless, the management refused to recognise the union, changing the company's name first to Harris Solid State Malaysia (HSSM) and later again to Harris Advanced Technology in order to thwart the workers' efforts. All the workers have eventually been absorbed into the new company while the union leaders have been effectively dismissed. The case is still pending.

CONCLUSION

As Malaysia came to the fore as one of the new generation NICs in the aftermath of structural adjustment, its society is increasingly integrated into the global materialist culture.[38] In general, incomes have risen, the standard of living is higher and there is heightened consumerism. This growing materialist and consumerist culture penetrates all layers of urban Malaysian society,[39] including the women workers who are the subject of our discussion. Foo and Lim (1989) have lucidly discussed how this consumerism is part of a growing modern ideology of individual freedom which works in tandem with the existing gender ideology of women's role as secondary income earner, to subvert the development of class consciousness among Malaysian women factory workers.[40] Seen in the context of the superiority of factory employment for women, existing gender inequalities in Malaysian society, and the backwardness of the rural sector, they argue, it is rational for women to subscribe to these ideologies.

Convincing though their arguments are, they none the less seem to neglect two important actors who cannot but play important roles in women workers' subjective consciousness. First is the Malaysian state, which exerts control and dominance over society in many direct and indirect ways, including the institutionalisation and perpetuation of ethnic ideology and consciousness, and the setting up of coercive and repressive labour legislation which works against the development of labour organisations. Second are the management and owners of capital, who not only exploit and repress labour, but also use many different tactics to fragment workers and undermine their unity.

Large numbers of women workers in the export-oriented manufacturing industries are part of an exodus from the rural to the urban areas which began when new employment opportunities were made available to the Malays under the New Economic Policy of 1970.[41] At present, Malaysia's economy is expanding further, making possible multiple sources of income for the family. Moreover, in this era of rapid industrialisation, modernisation and changes in class formation,[42] social mobility may take place within one generation.

Ethnic ideology is very pervasive, and ethnic divisions in society are very sharp. The state perpetuates the idea that it has been the sole benefactor of the Malays who, without state support, would not have been able to compete with the other ethnic groups, in particular the Chinese. In this context, factory employment for young Malay women, which provides an additional source of family income, is seen as part of the state's efforts to raise the standard of living of the rural Malays.

The state also exercises ideological hegemony over civil society through its control over the education system, the media[43] and cultural and religious activities. Where this fails, it resorts to a set of coercive legislation – such as the Internal Security Act, Official Secrets Act, Sedition Act, Printing Act, Societies Act, University and University Colleges Act – all of which serve to restrict civil liberties. Repressive labour legislation is part of this battery of coercive laws. As industrialisation progresses and competition becomes keener, it becomes more and more necessary to keep labour pliant and under control in order to keep labour costs down and maintain Malaysia as a haven for foreign investment.

In this chapter, we have discussed extensively some of the new organisations of work which appeared with new technology and economic restructuring, and their effects on women workers. New technologies – leading to automation and computerisation – do not by themselves intensify work or suppress workers. Nevertheless, in the present political and economic system, there are no checks and balances on what management can do to squeeze higher and higher levels of productivity from the workers, to the detriment of their physical health, social and mental well-being and long-term security. As we have explained, shiftwork and overtime not only affect the health of workers, but also force them to structure their daily lives around the factory, allowing them little time for leisure activities, much less for organising. Incentive schemes based upon individual performance act to divide women workers; while human resource management techniques such as quality control circles are used to inculcate a sense of company loyalty.

Yet, in spite of the combined might of the state and the owners of capital, workers have managed to organise spontaneous strike actions. Admittedly, spontaneous strikes are not a high form of organisation, and usually cannot be sustained over a protracted period. Nevertheless, they do indicate a certain level of consciousness of the power of unity and concerted action by workers.

NOTES

1 Structural adjustment, strictly referring to the World Bank and International Monetary Fund economic restructuring and stabilisation programmes, did not occur in Malaysia. Many of the features in the economic restructuring that the Malaysian government undertook in the 1980s, however, are similar to measures recommended by the two institutions. In this chapter, the term 'structural adjustment' when applied to Malaysia is used to refer to the economic restructuring which took place largely from the mid-1980s onwards.

2 The office workers study was carried out in PUBS, a public sector agency; TELMAL, a telecommunications company; MANAS, an airline company; and BANKAM, a local bank. Over 1,000 workers took part in a questionnaire interview, group interviews and in-depth interviews. Interviews with women electronics workers were carried out for a paper on occupational health and safety of electronics workers (Manohary and Chee, 1992). In addition, we conducted a group discussion with nine workers who live in a rural village and work in a small Taiwanese factory.

3 The economic boom resulting from postwar economic reconstruction lasted for twenty-five years. It petered out in the 1960s and 1970s, and

this set the stage for the global economic crisis of the 1980s (Jomo, 1990: 16–20).

4 This is done in the aftermath of the 1969 race riots, which had led to the New Economic Policy with its twin objectives of eradicating poverty and restructuring the Malaysian economy so as to abolish the identification of occupation with ethnicity. Export-oriented industries were expected to create jobs which would preferably be given to Malays. See Suresh and Rajah (1992) for a discussion of this aspect of Malaysia's industrialisation strategy.

5 This was concentrated in a small number of countries, establishing points of access to primary resources and points of distribution for manufactured commodities (Sussman, 1989: 282–283). For example, by 1978 twenty countries received 75 per cent of the total relocated investment; while eight countries, including the NICs, received three-quarters of all foreign direct investment in Third World Asia between 1971 and 1978 (ibid.: 282). Between 1980 and 1990, ten countries, five of them NICs, accounted for almost 70 per cent of the foreign direct investment flows to developing countries (Padman, 1993).

6 Some believe that the government did not want to cut government expenditure before the 1982 general elections; others say the increased government spending was due to Tengku Razaleigh's (the then Finance Minister) Keynesian approach, while Daim (who succeeded him in 1984) is associated with structural adjustment measures.

7 Indeed, despite the 1983 privatisation policy, the public sector's share of total investments was higher in the 1980s than in the 1960s and 1970s (Jomo, 1990: 46). Real private investment grew by 10.6 per cent in 1984, fell by 8.1 per cent in 1985 and by 18.3 per cent in 1986, before growing again by 39.9 per cent in 1987 and 14.7 per cent in 1988. In contrast, public sector investment grew by 41.5 per cent in 1981, 20.7 per cent in 1982, and 10.2 per cent in 1983, before being trimmed by 4.4 per cent in 1984, 11 per cent in 1985, 18.5 per cent in 1986 and 10.7 per cent in 1987 (Jomo, 1990: 50–51).

8 These figures are believed to be underestimates, especially in sectors where contract labour is used (Jomo, 1990: 85).

9 For an extensive discussion of the measures the Malaysian government took to liberalise the investment climate after 1986, refer to Johan (1991: 8–15).

10 The first consists of twenty-two volumes, of which only fifteen have been released to the public. This contrasts with the thirteen-page National Agricultural Policy released in early 1984 (Jomo, 1990: 134).

11 The manufacturing sector, for example, is heavily dominated by electronics and electrical products and textiles and garments, which together accounted for 65 per cent of manufactured exports in 1983. Semiconductor assembly alone accounted for 41 per cent. Furthermore, the output of the electronics industry, the leading sub-sector in manufacturing, is 80–85 per cent components, as opposed to industrial or consumer electronics, and even within components production, semiconductor assembly and testing constitutes between 83–92 per cent of the output (Jomo, 1990: 136–137).

12 This may be an overestimate as foreign labour is not taken into account in official figures. There are an estimated 1.6 million foreign workers (out of this, 0.5 million are in Sabah and Sarawak) in Malaysia, representing about 20 per cent of the labour force (Jomo, 1990: 219).

13 This is in contrast with the situation in 1985–1986, when collective agreements were able to win wage increments of between 2–3 per cent only. The Finance Minister's 1987 budget speech recommended a three-year wage freeze (Jomo, 1990: 89).

14 The country is presently facing an energy crisis, while the Malaysian International Chamber of Commerce and Industry revealed that the water supply situation in the Kelang Valley has reached a critical stage. Datuk Seri Rafidah Aziz, Minister of International Trade and Industry, was quoted as saying that the infrastructure crisis reflects 'our inability to manage our success' (Raj, 1993).

15 From 1984 to 1987, household incomes fell slightly in real terms. The incidence of urban poverty increased slightly even though the incidence of rural poverty continued to decrease, albeit at a slower rate than before (Demery and Demery, 1992: 25).

16 In the agricultural sector, rural development programmes have served to marginalise women on the one hand, and mechanisation has served to displace women's labour on the other. Rural women emigrate to urban centres to work in the manufacturing industries or commute daily, in some cases travelling for up to three hours. Factory jobs are welcomed because they ensure stable incomes, higher on average than those of poor peasant families.

17 In 1987, Malaysia was ranked the fourth largest user of computers – after Japan, Singapore and Hong Kong.

18 'If I do shiftwork, I can survive with my allowance and the overtime. Then I can send money home and use some for myself too. If you do only normal shift, it is difficult. My basic pay is only $335, but with the allowances added on, I can get $500. I send home $100. I have to pay $60 for the room itself [union-subsidised housing].' (Interview with Safiah, Petaling Jaya, 1992)

19 Absenteeism is aggravated by workers having to work unpopular shifts. To take an excerpt from an interview with a woman worker in a large multinational company, 'They had a lot of problems with girls taking MCs (medical certificates) or annual leave to be off on a Saturday night, because they want to go out. So they started giving gifts to workers if, in one quarter, they do not take any MCs.' (Interview with Sheila, Petaling Jaya, 1992)

20 This is a large Japanese multinational company which manufactures various electronics components. It has a complex of four factories located in an industrial area in the Kelang Valley. The company runs a five-day week covering 365 days in a year. The two shifts are from 7.30 a.m. to 5.03 p.m. and from 9.27 p.m. to 7.05 a.m. The period in between, that is, from 5.03 p.m. to 9.27 p.m. is covered by overtime work; so is Saturday and Sunday. This kind of arrangement is made possible by a high level of automation. The management is quick to stress that the company abides by Malaysian law which sets the maximum hours that a

worker can work at sixty-four per week, and that each worker gets the minimum of ten public holidays per year. (Briefing during visit to factory, Shah Alam, February 1993)

21 'We work in three shifts. Before, we used to do two weeks for every shift. Two weeks in the morning (6 a.m.–2 p.m.), then two weeks nights (10 p.m.–6 a.m.), and then two weeks afternoons (2 p.m.–10 p.m.). Now, it is one week per shift. There are four crews – A, B, C and D – that work on a rotating basis. You work six full days, then you get two days' rest. This means that there is no stop in the factory. It was started two years ago. Before, we used to get every Sunday off. Now, we only get Saturdays and Sundays off every one and a half months. This is difficult because our rest days do not coincide with our family's. We also don't like the afternoon shift because when our families and friends come home from work, we are at work. You miss out a lot on social activities. After every night shift it takes me two to three days to adjust. I cannot sleep at night, and I have bad headaches.' (Interview with Sheila, Petaling Jaya, 1992)

22 'The supervisor frightens us about the work audit where we are questioned about our work process. It is like an interview. And if we do not know how to answer the questions, then there is no increment. He also asks us how many reject ppm [i.e. per time unit] and if we can't answer then the bonus is less. Different workers are paid differently. Many workers who take leave have their bonuses cut. All this frightens the workers.' (Interview with Safiah, Petaling Jaya, 1992)

23 Governmental repression and underhand management tactics are of course overriding reasons. The intensity of work and the organisation of work around shifts require that workers virtually structure their life around their jobs, and leave precious little time for leisure, much less organising.

24 'Before, one person takes care of one machine. Then, they gave two machines to one worker. Even to take care of one is already so difficult. First, they tell us that using the two machines is training. Then they say, since you can do it, continue.' (Interview with Sares, Bangi, 1992)

'Now they are checking to see how fast I can work. I can only do 3,000 a day, but when the technical engineer stands there to watch me, I can do so much more, maybe a thousand more. I am so scared that I quicken my pace. Then they comment and say, "So you can do so much but you don't do because you have been talking". They stand at the back of us and time how fast we can finish one product. Now our target has been increased from 10,000 to 16,000. It takes six to seven minutes to do [one process] but now I am told to do it in two minutes. But it is difficult because we have to check this, check that. I told the supervisor that I can't do it, but he keeps telling me that I can.' (Interview with Mani, Bangi, 1992)

25 'Lunch break is thirty minutes and tea break is fifteen minutes. If we are even one minute late, we are scolded. The supervisor would say that we can do at least one product in one minute. We can go to the toilet for up to twenty minutes, but then we will lose on targets.' (Interview with Norita, Petaling Jaya, 1992)

'Now the discipline is very controlled. We must wear the smock and a fully covered face mask. The bunny suit will be introduced to us soon. Some departments are already using it and the women are complaining. It's difficult to go to the toilet. You can only identify people by the colour of their smock. . . . Where time is concerned, workers have to be very punctual. Before, we could be five minutes late, or take five minutes more than the given time for breaks, but not any more. Last time there was freedom we could go to another line, see a friend. But now, it is very strict. . . . Last time, the line was wide open. You could see all your friends but now you can't. They have blocked off department by department. Before, we know who works where. Now, some areas we cannot go in unless we are authorised.' (Interview with Lina, Petaling Jaya, 1992)

26 'I thought that working with the computer was the best. That is why I applied to this place. This is like working in a factory. I cannot talk to my neighbour, I cannot rest, I cannot go to the toilet, I cannot write during my rest time. I cannot even use the phone' (Ng, 1992: 25).

27 'There are now more restrictions. We cannot take an afternoon tea break; there are specific times for breaks. We cannot relax as people are eyeing you, or we are afraid that others are eyeing you. There is now more pressure to work' (Ng, 1992: 26).

28 The same factory as in note 20.

29 'Now I work in the solder department. I suffer from bad headaches, eye tearing and eye pain. I found out that it's the solder fumes that are giving me the problems. The solder fumes are so bad, they come straight into my face. I tear so much, and I cannot work without using eye glasses.' (Interview with Rani, Kajang, 1992)

'In this [die-bond] section, I worked with epoxy. It is white in colour. My hands could not take it. The skin on my palms began to crack and bleed. Even if I wear gloves, it still bleeds. I have been suffering from it for two years. It takes a long time to heal. I could not use my hands to do anything.' (Interview with Devi, Kajang, 1992)

30 'Women do not last very long in the mould room. They did a research. The girls resign, and they always have to recruit new girls. It takes a lot of time to train them. They are given an allowance of $10 a day in addition to their daily wage of $7.50. This was started in 1991. They have to wear a cap, face mask, safety glasses, smock, and thick gloves for safety. This was given in 1989, after many women in this department died of cancer. . . . It was a shock to hear that the mould room girl died. It was impossible to believe. I was scared and the other girls working in the mould room were also scared. But now, no more, because "money talks". They have allowances, so they don't bother about being sick. If you work in the mould room, you are given a medical check-up every year. The other workers go for a check-up only once in three or four years. Every damn thing they will check. It is all fate. But we take precautions [referring to the masks]. If you want to live very long, you will be scared.' (Interview with Sal, Shah Alam, 1992)

31 'The woman who died of lung cancer in that department did not want a transfer when she was having symptoms because she did not think it

could be serious. Once the management knows that you are sick they will medically board you out. The management people went to the hospital themselves and talked to the patient. The company paid the family and told them not to talk about it any more. This worker was a healthy woman.' (Interview with Sal, Shah Alam, 1992)

32 'When I first started using the scope, I see the things moving in circles, and I feel like vomiting all the time. I suffer from constant headaches and feel as though someone is pushing my head hard to the back.... Now, it is worse. Inside the scope, they have put a light. When I look at it, I feel as though the light goes into my head. When I look into the scope, then I look up, it is blur. The supervisor says the light is to help to see the rejects clearly. But when I look, it is glaring. I said, "The light is dangerous to health", but the supervisor replied, "Surely it is dangerous, but no one has died from using the scope." What more to say? He is the supervisor, I am only an operator. . . . When I see the doctor, he says that I am strange. "When you watch TV, do you have headache?" He is making fun of me. Friends say, if you really cannot work, why don't you go home? But what am I going to do at home?' (Interview with Norita, Petaling Jaya, 1992)

33 'Shift work gives us a lot of problems. It takes a whole week to recover from one shift but soon the other shift comes. If you don't have enough sleep you can fall sick. I have gastritis because of irregular meals. After thirteen years I am still not used to it. It makes me restless and tired. When it comes to the night shift I hardly eat. Most of the time I don't eat the whole day, sometimes I even skip breakfast. I can't sleep and it's not the same as sleeping during the night. I only sleep one or two hours during night shift. Married women like to do night shift because they can be at home during the day with their children.' (Interview with Banu, Petaling Jaya, 1992)

34 It was revealed during a briefing by the personnel manager during a visit to an electronics factory (the same one as in note 11) that the latest mass hysteria among the workers happened six months ago. The visit was conducted in February. There was nothing in the local papers about this event.

35 An official count in 1993 reports 80,000 migrant workers registered with the Immigration Department of Malaysia, and another 230,000 registered but awaiting work permits. Official counts mask the presence of at least an estimated one million illegal migrant workers in the country. Given a labour force of eight million workers, one million foreign workers is a significant force in the country (Ng, 1993).

36 In 1988, for example, out of 322 union presidents, only 13 (4 per cent) were women. Out of 322 secretaries, 23 (7.1 per cent) were women, and out of 322 treasurers, 33 (10.2 per cent) were women (Rohana, 1992: 132).

37 Only a few are mentioned here. Like the occurrence of mass hysteria, there must be smaller protest actions which have either escaped the attention of reporters, or deemed unnewsworthy by newspaper editors.

38 Some of the ideas in this section are drawn from Johan et al. (1992) and Johan (1991).

39 It even reaches rural communities through the widespread availability of television and radio sets, increased mobility, and urbanites whose families and relatives are still living in rural areas.

40 They argue that the women workers want to work in the factories, not out of absolute poverty, but because they want to be independent, to have autonomy – in particular, consumer autonomy, and so that they have money to give to their parents (an expression of the traditional family ideology of parental repayment – the idea is that since our parents brought us up, it is only fair that we repay them in some way). On the other hand, the idea that they will stop working once they get married, or that, as wives, their incomes are supplementary to their husbands', results in a weak commitment to the labour force and hence the lack of development of class consciousness.

41 Most women production operators in the modern manufacturing industries are Malays and Indians; the proportion of Chinese is very small, and they generally occupy the higher positions.

42 Specifically, the New Economic Policy (NEP) has largely succeeded in creating a substantial Malay middle class.

43 All television and radio networks are owned by the state, while the major newspapers and the only private television station are owned by government political parties.

REFERENCES

Commonwealth Secretariat (1993) 'Overview of Major Issues'. Paper presented at the Asian Regional Seminar on Structural Adjustment, Economic Change and Women. Kuala Lumpur, 5–8 January.

Demery, D. and Demery, L. (1992) 'Adjustment and Equity in Malaysia', in C. Morrison (ed.) *Adjustment and Equity in Developing Countries*, Paris: Development Centre of the Organisation for Economic Cooperation and Development.

Devaraj, K. (1989) 'Logging Accidents in Sarawak', in *Logging Against the Natives of Sarawak*, Petaling Jaya, Malaysia: INSAN.

Elson, D. (1993) 'Gender and Adjustment in the 1990s: An Update on Evidence and Strategies'. Paper presented at the Asian Regional Seminar on Structural Adjustment, Economic Change and Women, Kuala Lumpur, 5–8 January.

Foo, G. H. C. and Lim, L. Y. C. (1989) 'Poverty, Ideology and Women Export Factory Workers in South-East Asia', in H. Afshar and B. Agarwal (eds) *Women, Poverty and Ideology in Asia*, London: Macmillan.

HAWA (Hal–Ehwal Wanita, Women's Affairs Division, Ministry of National Unity and Social Development) (1993) 'Structural Adjustment in the Malaysian Economy and Implications on the Role of Women in Development'. Paper Presented at the Asian Regional Seminar on Structural Adjustment, Economic Change and Women, Kuala Lumpur, 5–8 January.

Jayaweera, S. (1993) 'Asian Experience on Structural Adjustment, Economic

Change and Women: Background Paper'. Paper presented at the Asian Regional Seminar on Structural Adjustment, Economic Change and Women, Kuala Lumpur, 5–8 January.

Johan, S. (1991) 'Industrialisation and the Institutionalisation of Authoritarian Political Regimes: The Consequences of NICdom in Malaysia and Singapore', International Peace Research Institute Meigaku (PRIME), Occasional papers series no. 8.

Johan, S., Muhammad Ikmal Said, Loh Kok Wah et al. (1992) 'Malaysia: The Pitfalls of NICdom', in 'State of the Asian Peoples: A Report', *Asian Exchange* 8, 1/2: 13–46.

Jomo, K. S. (1990) 'Growth and Structural Change in the Malaysian Economy', in P. Nolan and M. Falkus (eds) *Studies in the Economies of East and South-East Asia*, London: Macmillan.

Khor, G. L. (1992) 'Occupational Health Problems in the Manufacturing Industries of Malaysia', in M. R. Reich and T. Okubo (eds) *Protecting Workers' Health in the Third World: National and International Strategies*, New York: Auburn House.

Lochead, J. (1987) 'Retrenchment in a Malaysian Free Trade Zone', in N. Heyzer (ed.) *Daughters in Industry*, Kuala Lumpur: Asia and Pacific Development Centre.

Malaysia (1989) 'Mid-Term Review of the Fifth Malaysia Plan, 1986–1990', Kuala Lumpur: National Printing Department.

—— (1991) *Sixth Malaysia Plan, 1991–1995*, Kuala Lumpur: National Printing Department.

Manohary, S. and Chee, H. L. (1992) 'Health and Safety Problems of Electronics Factory Workers: Workers' Perspectives'. Paper presented at the Conference on Safety and Health in Electronics, Persatuan Sahabat Wanita and Women's Development Collective, Petaling Jaya, Malaysia, 4–5 December.

Nash, J. (1988) 'Women in the World Capitalist Crisis'. Paper presented at the Conference on Feminism and Anthropology, University of Amsterdam, 12–13 December.

National Office for Human Development (1993) 'National Report on Filipino Migrant Workers in Malaysia'. Paper presented at the Symposium on Filipino Migrant Workers in Asia, 11–18 September, Kuala Lumpur: National Office for Human Development.

Ng, C. Choon Sim (1992) *Office Automation in Malaysia: The Case of the Telecommunications Industry*, Working paper series 132, The Hague: Institute for Social Studies.

Ng, C. Choon Sim and Othman, J. (1992) 'IT and Gender Differences among Office Workers in Malaysia', in S. C. Bhatnagar and M. Odedra (eds) *Social Implications of Computers in Developing Countries*, New Delhi: Tata McGraw-Hill.

Padman, P. (1993) 'Curbing Dumping, Double Standards', *New Straits Times*, 6 March.

Raj, C. (1993) 'Time for Industries to Get their Act Together', *New Straits Times*, 6 March.

Rajah, R. (1992) 'Malaysian Electronics: History and Current Developments'. Paper presented at the Conference on Safety and Health in

Electronics, Persatuan Sahabat Wanita and Women's Development Collective, Petaling Jaya, Malaysia, 4–5 December.

Rohana, A. (1991) 'The Participation of Women in Trade Unions in Peninsular Malaya with Special Reference to MTUC and CUEOACS'. Unpublished Ph.D. thesis, Faculty of Sociology and Anthropology, University of Malaya.

Suresh, N. and Rajah, R. (1992) 'Malaysian Electronics: The Changing Prospects of Employment and Restructuring', *Development and Change* 23, 4: 75–99.

Sussman, G. (1989) 'Singapore's Niche in the New International Division of Information', in P. Limqueco (ed.) *Partisan Scholarship: Essays in Honour of Renato Constantino*, Manila and Wollongong: JCA Publishers.

8

TARGETING WOMAN-HEADED HOUSEHOLDS AND WOMAN-MAINTAINED FAMILIES IN DEVELOPING COUNTRIES

Mayra Buvinić and Geeta Rao Gupta

INTRODUCTION

This chapter examines the question of the desirability and effectiveness of targeting public and private sector interventions to a subset of households and individuals who experience some of the more extreme forms of economic and social insecurity in developing countries. That is, women who head households or who maintain families in developing countries. The assumption is that these women are trebly disadvantaged:

> As *poor people*, they live under the same harsh conditions as their male counterparts; as *women*, they suffer from cultural and policy biases which undervalue their contribution to development and prevent them from increasing the productivity of their labour; and as *heads of households*, they face the same problems while having to carry out the full burden of household management and production for which they get very little support.
>
> (Jazairy, Alamgir and Panuccio, 1992: 273–274)

Thus, our contribution to this volume addresses the first of the two questions posed in the Introduction – on the impact of women of global transformations – and evaluates the potentials and pitfalls of a given policy, aimed at a specific, and extremely vulnerable, category of women.

It is important to stress at the outset, however, that the source of the potential insecurity of woman-maintained households in developing countries is probably quite unrelated to the retreat of the state – simply because the state has seldom even recognised and benefited them. Developing-country policies have been blind to gender concerns and especially to the problems of female heads. This blindness can be attributed both to ignorance and to the anticipated political costs of implementing gender policies, which can be perceived as unusually high in the case of policies targeted to female-headed households.

This chapter examines potential costs and benefits of targeting female headship and uses this analysis as the framework to review both the experience of public works programmes that benefit poor female heads and the experiences of two countries, Chile and India, that have deviated from the norm and have targeted female headship through the state. The objective is to illustrate interventions by the state that could counter the extreme economic and social insecurity of many poor women and their families, but within a realistic gender-analysis framework that anticipates and examines costs and benefits that can affect implementation.

We precede the analysis of costs and benefits and the review of targeted interventions by examining the relationship between female headship and poverty to establish an empirical basis for arguing for the potential insecurity of these families. Before examining the evidence, we need to insert a note on terminology. The problems with defining and measuring woman-headed households are well known. Cultural differences and industrialised-country assumptions about families cloud the identification of female headship. Reliable identification of these households is further compounded by the facts that female headship may be a transitory phenomenon in the life-cycle of families and that there is an important distinction between woman-headed households (residential units) and woman-maintained families (kin-ship units). A woman-maintained family may, as a sub-family, reside in a larger, often male-headed household. A third and perhaps most serious limitation is that the term 'head of household' is not neutral. It is loaded with additional meanings that reflect a traditional emphasis on households as undifferentiated units with a patriarchal system of governance and no internal conflicts in the allocation of resources (Folbre, 1991).

Despite these definitional problems, we believe that the term 'female headship' is useful for purposes of programme and policy implementation, but we stress the need to recognise as well the existence of woman-maintained families who often reside as sub-families in larger households. Woman-headed households and woman-maintained families, we propose, are practical, albeit imper-fect, proxies for a whole range of family structures exposed to economic and social insecurities because women are the primary economic providers for the family.

THE POVERTY AND VULNERABILITY OF FEMALE-HEADED HOUSEHOLDS

The relationship between female headship and poverty and the consequences of female headship in terms of the vulnerability of future generations have been reasonably well studied. We reviewed information from sixty-five studies, carried out in the past decade. Sixteen were done in Africa, seventeen in Asia and thirty-two in Latin America and the Caribbean. Self-report and the physical absence of men due to migration, death, divorce or abandonment were the most commonly used definitions of female headship in the studies. Some studies distinguished between *de facto* and *de jure* female headship, and a few examined the situation of functional families headed by women residing in larger households.

Relationship to poverty

Of the sixty-five studies reviewed, sixty-one have examined the relationship of female headship to poverty. Thirty-eight of the sixty-one studies find that woman-headed households are over-represented among the poor by using a variety of poverty indicators: total or per capita income, mean income per adult equivalence, total or per capita consumption of expenditures, access to services, and ownership of land and assets, among others. Fifteen other studies found that poverty was associated with certain types of female heads, or that the association emerged for certain poverty indicators. Only eight of the sixty-one studies (13 per cent) showed no empirical evidence for the hypothesis of the greater poverty of female-headed households.

The studies that show a relationship between female headship and poverty point to three sets of factors that determine the greater poverty of woman-headed households. They emerge, respectively, from characteristics of household composition, the gender of the main earner, and the unique circumstance of being a woman-headed household.

Dependency burden

Woman-headed households, despite their smaller size in comparison to other types of households, often carry a higher dependency burden. That is, they tend to contain a higher ratio of non-workers to workers than do other households, as supported by data from rural Botswana, Malawi, Brazil, Mexico and Peru (Kossoudji and Mueller, 1983; Berheide and Segal, 1989; Merrick and Schmink, 1983; Rosenhouse, 1988).

This type of household composition would not necessarily lead to poverty, however, if the household received child-support payments from absent fathers, as is the case with some of the left-behind rural female heads in India who receive adequate remittances (Gulati, 1983; Jain, 1989). The poverty of woman-headed households thus reflects a disruption of traditional systems of family governance that enforced income transfers from fathers to children (Folbre, 1991).

Gender-related economic gap

The main earners of woman-headed families are by definition women, who have lower average earnings than men, fewer assets and less access to remunerative jobs and productive resources, such as land, capital and technology. This gender-related economic gap contributes to the economic vulnerability of woman-headed families. In Brazil, female-headed households have a 30–50 per cent greater chance of being in poverty than male-headed ones, not because they have more children or fewer adults, but because the female head earns less. The lower earning power of women heads of household was a function of their lower education in Peru (Tienda and Salazar, 1980) and of their restricted access to land and credit in El Salvador (Lastarria-Cornheil, 1988) and in villages in India (Jain, 1989).

This second set of factors, then, emerges from gender differences in access to economic opportunities. It follows that the implementation of policies that expand economic opportunities for all women should reduce the vulnerability to poverty of woman-headed households.

Other factors

Some of the reasons for the higher poverty of woman-maintained families cannot be attributed to household structure factors *per se* nor, strictly, to gender-related differences in economic opportunity, but to

135

the combination of both. That is, there is an independent effect of female headship on household economic vulnerability that cannot be reduced to the characteristics of women or the household. This effect, in turn, can operate through three different mechanisms. First, women who are heads of households and have no other (female) adult help also have to fulfil home production or domestic roles. They therefore face greater time and mobility constraints than male heads and other women, which can result in an apparent 'preference' for working fewer hours for pay, for 'choosing' lower-paying jobs that are nevertheless more compatible with childcare, and for spending more for certain services, such as water and housing, because they cannot contribute time to offset transaction costs. Chipande (1987) describes how women farmers in Malawi were inclined to limit their labour time in farm activities due to a heavy commitment to domestic chores. Berheide and Segal (1989) and Kossoudji and Mueller (1983) report similar findings. They found that responsibility for children and housekeeping made it difficult for female heads to opt for regular or off-farm labour activities to increase their earnings.

Second, women who head households may encounter discrimination in access to jobs or resources beyond that which they encounter because of their gender or may themselves, because of social or economic pressures, make inappropriate choices that affect the household's economic welfare. In Chile, for instance, Schkolnik (1991) found that female heads had significantly less access to government subsidies than other heads. Third, female heads may have a history of premature parenthood and family instability that tends to perpetuate poverty to succeeding generations.

The weight of the evidence reviewed, therefore, indicates that female-headed families with children to support tend to be disproportionately represented among the poor. The exceptions include situations where there is a tradition of women living apart from husbands and the older generation (such as when female-headed families are embedded in the culture of matrilineal societies in West Africa, for instance), when women with economic means choose such families, and when absent partners send adequate remittances. There are many social and economic situations that predispose certain family types to poverty, and these may be highly culture-bound. For instance, out-of-wedlock teenage childbearing is a major predisposing factor in most Latin American countries and in some African countries, while in India early widowhood is far more important. Researchers need to investigate the relative contribution of the different factors in generating female-headed families and in determining their poverty to design appropriate and effective interventions.

The transmission of disadvantage

A most persuasive rationale for targeting female headship is to reduce the transmission of poverty into the next generation. In the twenty-nine studies we reviewed, when the indicators of disadvantage are children's nutritional status and school performance, female headship sometimes seems to protect against poverty, and at other times reproduce it. There is a slight bias towards finding more protective effects in Africa, but recent studies report this phenomenon also in Latin America and the Caribbean (Buvinić et al., 1992; Engle, 1991 and 1993; Johnson and Rogers, 1993).

Children's nutrition

There are varying results from the studies that have examined nutritional effects on children. Of the eighteen studies that examined nutritional effects, roughly half reported positive and half reported negative effects of female headship. Kumar's (1991) study from Zambia and Garcia's (1991) study from the Philippines found that a greater percentage of children in woman-headed households were malnourished as compared with children from other households. Wood (1989) found that the survival probabilities of children in woman-headed households in Brazil were significantly lower than those of children in male-headed households. This difference in child mortality was not the result of female headship *per se*, but rather was the outcome of differences in race, region, education, housing quality, monthly household income and other standard of living indicators. Similarly, Brazilian children of female-headed households were more likely to work, but this was accounted for by characteristics associated with the lower income and living standards of households with female heads (Levison, 1989).

The studies found that when 'peeling the onion' (or controlling for variables associated with female headship), the negative effect of headship on child welfare disappeared. This outcome implies that, at least in Brazil, female headship *per se* does not add extra burdens to being a woman or being black and, therefore, would argue for less targeted measures to attack the inter-generational poverty trans-mitted by female headship.

Studies that report a positive effect of female headship on child nutrition find this effect to be more significant in poorer than in better-off households (Kennedy, 1992; Engle, 1991; Buvinić et al., 1992). The more credible explanation for the positive effect is that there are gender differences in expenditure preferences (whether this preference results from nature or nurture – see Fuchs (1989) – is immaterial in terms of policy). This explanation rests on the notion that a woman's greater preference to invest in children is more easily realised in a household she heads, where there are no conflicts or negotiations with a male partner over the use of household resources. This preference appears in poorer families rather than in better-off ones, either because investments in children yield greater returns at lower levels of income, or because there are fewer competing alternative investments than in higher-income households (Kennedy, 1992).

The gender preference explanation receives support from research that finds similar effects when analysing unearned income of mothers who are not female heads (Thomas, 1990). An alternative explanation is that more competent mothers have more success at earning a higher proportion of family income, living on their own, and caring for their children.

Children's education

Of the studies that examined the impact of female headship on children's education, four report positive effects: that children's education is more likely to receive priority in woman-headed households than in male-headed households (Chernichowsky and Smith, 1979; Chant, 1985; Gulati, 1983; Louat, Grosh and van der Gaag, 1992). Six reported a negative effect: because of the lack of labour and low-income levels in households headed by women, children are often forced to drop out of school to assist in housework and childcare (Paes de Barros, Fox and Pinto de Mendonca, 1993; Vial, Muchnik and Kain, 1988; Kumari, 1989; Kazi and Raza, 1989; DeGraff and Bilsborrow, 1993; Schwede, 1991). These results are not necessarily contradictory. It is more likely that they represent evidence of the conflict that women heads of household must face; that is, the need to use every available resource to survive, versus a desire to invest in their children. The same can be argued for the observation of both protective and high-risk effects of female headship on child nutrition. That is, the protective effects from gender-

138

related preferences are likely to break down with increasing impoverishment.

Overall, the evidence suggests that poor woman-headed households prefer to invest scarce resources in children, which translates into increased child welfare relative to income. When women have access to insufficient income they cannot act on their 'preferences' sufficiently to make up the difference. In this latter case, the economic deprivation that they suffer is transmitted to the next generation. While the primary mediation for the reproduction of poverty appears to be economic, some evidence from Latin America suggests that the absence of fathers may transmit social as well as economic disadvantages to the next generation, either directly by their absence or indirectly by affecting the caretaking behaviour of mothers and other child-rearing agents (Engle, 1993; Buvinić et al., 1992).

COSTS AND BENEFITS OF TARGETING FEMALE HEADSHIP

Targeting anti-poverty interventions has become an increasingly popular practice given the pressure of governments to reduce public expenditure and the failure of much of past social spending by governments to actually reach the poor. By targeting, governments expect to increase the cost-effectiveness of programmes and ensure that assistance reaches the most needy. A counterpoint to targeting is universalistic programmes that provide benefits paid independent of income, age or any other characteristic that defines a target group.

Selected populations are targeted when they have the problem, that is, when they are poor, or when they are highly vulnerable to acquiring the problem (becoming poor). People who are poor can be helped with direct or indirect transfers, while stabilisation, social insurance or safety nets are used to prevent or contain the risk of people becoming poor. In addition, programmes rather than populations can be selected for targeting. Effective interventions targeted to the poor in developing countries have included a number of alternatives. Following the criterion of targeting programmes rather than populations, food support schemes have been implemented to subsidise food consumed by the poor versus the rich, such as subsidies in the price of cassava versus wheat in Brazil (World Bank, 1990). Another form of food-related transfers are food stamps and food rations, which are more desirable politically than direct cash transfers and include substantially less leakages to the rich when compared to across-the-board food subsidies (Besley and Kanbur, 1990). Social welfare goods such as school meals programmes and nutrition interventions to pregnant and lactating mothers have also been successfully targeted (in Chile, for instance). Public work schemes have effectively targeted the poor in a number of developing countries. Lastly, direct cash transfers have been an alternative left mostly to developed countries with sophisticated means testing mechanisms.

The benefit to the poor of targeting transfers is the gross amount of the transfer minus participation costs. Transaction costs of participating include foregone income from alternative occupations in schemes that have a work requirement (Ravallion, 1991), and psychological costs as a result of the social stigma often attached to participation in programmes directed only to the poor (Besley and Kanbur, 1990). In the case of poor women, costs of participation can include alternative uses of time in home production and childcare, and costs derived form the social restrictions women often have on moving freely (i.e. to travel long distances) and interacting with men in public places.

For the government or the agency that finances targeting programmes, the costs of targeting include:

1 the cost of the goods or services delivered to the poor;
2 the amount of leakages to the non-poor as a result of errors in the screening process;
3 the administrative costs of the programme, which can be lowered when fewer indicators are used to identify the target population and when the basic infrastructure to deliver the good is in place;
4 political economy costs;
5 second-round costs or perverse incentive effects that are built into the nature of targeting intervention to some but not to all.

The more programmes target specific populations to the exclusion of others, the more these schemes are unsustainable politically. Targeting implies redistribution, which can create antagonism and result in the elimination of the programme; this is especially the case when the excluded population is more powerful than the targeted one – a condition that is always the case in anti-poverty schemes. Universal programmes, instead, have the main political advantage that in principle, at least, all share in the benefits. An example of the negative effects of targeting was the implementation of a food stamp programme in Sri Lanka to replace a universalistic food subsidy intervention. The programme was killed by the rich when they stopped benefiting (World Bank, 1990).

Anticipating costs and benefits: a gender analysis

The prevalence of female headship in developing countries varies substantially across countries and situations, comprising anywhere between 10 per cent to about 40 per cent of all households. From a purely budgetary perspective, the attractiveness of targeting female-headed households should increase when their prevalence is not too high, since interventions can be implemented at more reasonable costs with smaller targeted populations, particularly when it can be established that they are poorer and more vulnerable. There is logic to the argument that the more pervasive the problem, the greater is the case for resolving it with a universal programme (Garfinkel and McLanahan, 1986). Errors in screening woman-maintained households and families should be higher in terms of false negatives (that is, failing to capture households that are classified as male-headed when in reality they are woman-headed) than in terms of false positives. This is due to the increasing numbers of women who *de facto* maintain households in developing countries but are not recognised as such because of cultural prescriptions that identify the man as the main breadwinner and household authority (Buvinić, Youssef and von Elm, 1978). Shifting the target unit from woman-headed households to woman-headed families (that is, kinship units residing in larger households) should reduce the number of false negatives. The number of false positives (or leakages to men-headed households) may, nevertheless, increase with time. This is because over time women may shift in and out of the status of family head (by changing their marital status, for instance) and programmes that do not monitor benefits closely can end up providing benefits to some male-headed households that were formerly woman-headed. Programme designers should examine the empirical question of how easily the status of female headship may be altered. This ease should vary with the origins of female headship, women's physical and social mobility and the life-cycle stage of the family. *De facto* headship should in theory be more subject to change than *de jure* headship.

A second type of classification error occurs when woman-headed households are used as a proxy for poverty households and there are leakages to non-poor woman-headed households. In this case, the number of false positives (identifying as poor woman-headed households that are not) should decrease with the increasing proportion of female heads who are poor in the population. The likelihood of producing false negatives (failing to identify poor woman-headed households) should increase as the proportion of female heads who are poor declines.

Targeting woman-headed households and families may produce significant benefits to participating families and society, both direct and indirect. Targeting poor female heads will produce direct benefits for women if the gross amount of the benefit or transfer exceeds participation costs. The time costs of participating in a targeted intervention should be greater for these women than for men who head households or for women in male-headed households. In addition, participation costs arising from social mores may be higher for female heads than for other women (since in many cases a social stigma is attached to the condition of female headship). Targeting female headship may have larger benefits for children than targeting poor male-headed households with equal amounts of benefit. As an indirect or second-round benefit, targeting female headship can increase the fairness and effectiveness of development interventions. Another indirect benefit is making visible the unrecognised economic contribution of poor women.

The costs to society of targeting female-maintained families can be as large as the benefits, and high anticipated costs are likely to be one of the main reasons explaining why female headship has so seldom been targeted by government programmes. Any additional screening criteria impose administrative costs. Further, since targeting woman-headed families can imply excluding male-headed ones, there can be significant political costs – real or perceived. These costs should be substantially lower, however, if woman-headed families are targeted with women-specific interventions, such as nutrition supplements for pregnant women, maternal and child health interventions or training in female-specific occupations. Political considerations suggest avoiding the risk of antagonising the more powerful male constituency by targeting woman-headed families with resources that are not perceived as female-specific, such as housing subsidies, agricultural loans, food coupons and cash transfers. In addition, it suggests that targeting women who head families may be less politically viable than targeting all women. These political considerations do not bode well for the long-term survival of initiatives that target female headship with significant development resources.

Perhaps the major perceived cost of targeting woman-maintained families is the potential of changing the way families behave in response to programme incentives. Possible adverse incentive effects could include increasing the prevalence of female-headed households.

A dilemma may arise for programmes that target woman-headed families on the rationale of their poverty: do the short-term benefits of poverty relief compensate for the possible long-term increase in the prevalence of female-headed households?

THE EXPERIENCE OF TARGETING FEMALE HEADSHIP

Five governments have attempted to target female headship for poverty reasons: Barbados, Colombia, Chile, Honduras and India. The experiences of Chile and India are summarised below, following a review of employment schemes for the poor where self-targeting has attracted the participation of poor women and female heads.

Women's participation in employment programmes

A preferred strategy for targeting benefits to the poor has been public employment schemes that in principle are available to everyone ('universal') but offer sufficiently low wages to attract mostly the poor. The work requirements in these schemes imply costs to participants and build in the principle of self-targeting. The poor select themselves for participation and there is no need to establish restrictive criteria. The best known of these interventions is the Maharashtra Employment Guarantee Scheme (EGS) in India, which started in the early 1970s as an *ad hoc* public works programme and became a permanent programme in 1976. Public employment schemes set up to cope with economic recession are also well known in Bolivia, Chile and Peru.

The Maharashtra EGS programme, as well as Peru's Programma de Apoyo de Ingreso Temporal (PAIT) and the Programma de Empleo Mínimo (PEM) in Chile in the 1980s, attracted significant proportions of women workers and female heads of households. Somewhere between 38–50 per cent of those employed in the EGS scheme have been women (Ravallion, 1991; Acharya and Panwalkar, 1988). More than half of the workers of the PEM in Chile were women and they were three-quarters of the workers in the PAIT in Peru (World Bank, 1990).

Women's high participation rate is related to the low wage rate of these programmes. Programmes that provide market wages (such as Bolivia's emergency social fund and the POJH in Chile) have almost exclusively attracted male workers (Buvinić and Mellencamp, 1983;

World Bank, 1990). In fact, the Chilean government set up POJH as an explicit higher wage alternative for male heads of households and to discourage poor women from continuing to work outside the home.

Additional reasons why the Maharashtra EGS scheme has attracted women workers is because the sites have generally been within easy reach of the villages and childcare has been provided (Ravallion, 1991). An analysis of the Maharashtra programme in two villages, Shirapur and Kanzara, showed that woman-headed households had high participation rates (although the rates for females were lower than those for males). The presence of children did not reduce female participation rates – which could be a function of childcare provision (Deolalikar and Gaiha, 1992).

Some argue that women's predominance in the Maharashtra EGS is related to its non-discriminatory wage schedules. Participants are paid piece rates, independent of sex. In practice, however, different types of work receive different wages, and the jobs with higher wages are reserved for men. The *World Development Report*, for instance, documents the case of Laca, a woman participant in the Maharashtra scheme, and notes: 'Laca is rarely allowed to do the more strenuous and better-paid jobs, such as breaking rocks or digging irrigation tanks, although she knows she can do much of that kind of work' (World Bank, 1990: 99). The EGS, therefore, has been unable to bridge the gender wage gap in the labour market, but still it has provided poor women with an income generation option at low cost in terms of forgone income.

An additional reason to explain why women in economic need may flock towards these programmes is that women may be able to assume the psychological costs of programme participation better than men. In the Chile programme, social stigma was attached to participation in the lower-paid female-dominated PEM. This is one of the reasons why working-age men avoided it and preferred to participate in the higher-status, higher-wage POJH.

The experience of these programmes shows the willingness of poor women who maintain families to accept low-wage, low-status work. This experience also suggests that the programmes could incorporate features to reduce the gender gap in earnings, if this were an objective of public policy. Wages could be assigned on criteria other than hard physical (or men's) work; childcare could become a standard feature in these schemes; work could be based at home and parallel programmes with higher-wage rates could be avoided. Gender-informed public work programmes would be able to go far in alleviating women's poverty and correcting patterns of discrimination by sex.

Targeting poor woman-headed households in Chile

In 1991, after many congressional debates and significant opposition from conservative parties, the revived Chilean Congress approved a law that established the Women's National Service or Servicio Nacional de la Mujer (SERNAM). SERNAM is an autonomous agency attached directly to the presidency of the Republic. The director has ministerial rank. Opponents feared SERNAM would interfere in two major contentious social issues – Chile's standing prohibitions against divorce and abortion. SERNAM, however, has not involved itself in these controversial issues. Instead, it chose, as one of its priority programmes, to target poor woman-headed households in order to increase their incomes, improve the welfare of the members of these households, and end the discrimination between woman-headed households and male-headed households. This priority was fully endorsed by the government and met with no substantial opposition. Giving priority to poor women heads of household was a safe political alternative when compared with legislating on divorce or abortion.

The programme called for coordination between the different ministries to give preference to the children of woman-headed households in nutrition interventions and childcare; increase the economic opportunities of these women; expand their access to housing and information; and give preference in certain programmes to pregnant adolescents and adolescent mothers. Its most visible component was a comprehensive two-year pilot project launched in five municipalities known to have large proportions of poor households. The project targeted 500 woman-headed households in each municipality for a total of 2,500 (Valenzuela, 1992). The pilot project responded to the increasing problem of teenage childbearing and out-of-wedlock births and included in the target population single mothers with their children, even if they resided in a male-headed extended household.

The pilot project provided health services, job training, childcare, housing improvement and legal aid. It included some universal components, such as building infrastructure for childcare, as well as extending the hours of operation of health clinics (to all) to accommodate the time constraints of working female heads. Women household heads participating in the pilot project had priority access to these universal benefits. It emphasised a productive rather than a welfare orientation, offering no free hand-outs or direct cash transfers and requiring women to devote significant time to the project's training component. The pilot project relied on the infrastructure and services already in place in the chosen municipalities and included collaboration from government ministries as well as NGOs. It was financed by the state and international donors and was implemented through the municipalities. The pilot project has now become a national programme, and a priority programme within the government's strategies to combat poverty.

One of the participating municipalities was Conchalí, in Greater Santiago. Conchalí had about 200,000 inhabitants at the time and a progressive woman mayor who set up women-oriented programmes such as counselling on domestic violence and training local police to handle this issue. The Conchalí programme defined as woman-headed households, families with children under fourteen years of age as well as unwed or partnerless mothers and their children, even if the latter resided as sub-families in larger households. If a husband or partner was present, he had to be infirm, unemployed or unable to work. Aside from a small subsidy for transportation, the pilot project did not include direct cash transfers. The costs of participation were the time required to apply and participate in the different programmes offered. For instance, the vocational training courses required a total of 150 hours from each participant.

From a visit to Conchalí it became evident that the screening process was high in specificity (excluding those not in the target group) while sacrificing sensitivity (including all poor women heads). The main constraint was the time scheduled for screening. The screening was being offered in the afternoon, while many female heads (perhaps the neediest) were employed in menial work in professional cleaning services with long hours that were incompatible with applying for the programme. The social workers were aware of the time conflicts presented by the screening process, and were planning to have extended evening hours to register potential participants.

The women who applied that afternoon were mostly young, with children and with childcare conflicts, and expressed considerable interest in the combination of benefits the programme offered. The majority did not receive child support from the non-custodial father and had no plans to seek legal action to obtain it. A 28-year-old mother with two children – aged six and nine (who were left alone while she worked) – for instance, had not attempted to use legal means to get child support for fear of physical retaliation from the children's father.

While costs per participant were hard to estimate because some of the benefits were targeted while others are universal, we calculated overall project costs in Conchalí for the two-year project to be US$450 per woman per year, which is roughly similar to the costs per child per year of targeted nutritional interventions set at US$420 per year for a complementary feeding programme – PNAC (Vial, Muchnik and Kain, 1988). A survey of half of the beneficiaries carried out in 1992 showed that a full 91 per cent of the project participants had per capita family incomes below the poverty line (poorest 30 per cent), and 57 per cent were destitute (poorest 10 per cent). Only 0.2 per cent of the households fell among the non-poor. Only one other government programme (out of eleven) ranked higher than this project in terms of targeting benefits to the poor with very few leakages to the non-poor (Valenzuela, 1994).

If the pilot project is successful, however, a potentially much more serious criticism may arise. If the project succeeds in increasing the incomes of poor women heads, it may increase the prevalence of female headship by changing the living arrangements of unpartnered mothers and children now residing in somebody else's household. In 1992 one in five households in Chile had a sub-family residing in the household. More than half of these sub-families are headed by single mothers with children who would have the option of moving into independent housing. This has been one of the main effects of welfare programmes in the USA: to enable single mothers to establish independent residences (Garfinkel and McLanahan, 1986). Without this kind of analysis, it would be easy to mistakenly conclude that project benefits altered the costs and benefits of marriage for these unpartnered mothers, and that the government interfered, for the worse, in family life.

Targeting female-headed households in India

The government of India has repeatedly targeted particular groups for special benefits as a way to improve the social and economic status of vulnerable populations. In recent years women, and more specifically women-headed households, have been identified as targets for anti-poverty programmes. The government's seventh five-year plan for instance, draws attention to the 'single-parent rural family' as a

147

particularly vulnerable group and highlights the need to extend major rural development projects, such as the Integrated Rural Development Programme (IRDP), to households headed by women. The National Perspective Plan (NPP) for the years 1988 to 2000 also includes women-headed households as targets for various anti-poverty programmes.

In a paper prepared for the Population Council/ICRW joint Programme on Female Headship and Poverty, Devaki Jain (1992) discussed the pros and cons of targeting social and economic programmes to woman-headed households. Though Jain agreed that poor households headed by women deserve special benefits, she gave three reasons to question the effectiveness of targeting such households within the Indian context: an overemphasis on achieving numerical goals; the economic diversity of women-headed households; and difficulties in identifying appropriate households.

In India, the effectiveness of all targeted programmes tends to be judged by the extent to which they succeed in fulfilling predetermined quantitative goals. According to Jain, such a strategy for implementing welfare programmes can override selection criteria and leave the door wide open for bribery and corruption. 'The overriding pressure to achieve targets makes the system indifferent to the process – and the process is often more critical to goal achievement than the target' (Jain, 1992: 2).

An evaluation of anti-poverty programmes in Karnataka and Uttar Pradesh that targeted a quota of poor households, including woman-headed households, revealed similar problems (Krishnaswamy and Rajagopal, 1985). A large proportion of these programmes' benefits were diverted by local government officials to households who were not poor, in return for bribes. Thus, though Jain agreed that poor households headed by women deserved special benefits, she questioned whether targeting is the appropriate mechanism since the process of achieving targets is easily corruptible.

Jain's second argument was that, in the populations that she studied, woman-headed households were not always poor. In the Dakshina Kannada region of Karnataka, woman-headed households emerged from matrilineal descendance and were socially accepted and well-off, while the households headed by women in Uttar Pradesh were left behind by migrant males who sent adequate remittances home. In other regions, households headed by widows were sometimes poor and sometimes fairly economically stable. Moreover, the poor households headed by widows often did not have as high a dependency burden as poor households headed by men. Thus, Jain concluded that targeting woman-headed households for anti-poverty programmes is a flawed approach that may prevent interventions from reaching poor women residing in other households with higher dependency burdens.

Jain also discussed practical problems involved in identifying female household headship that makes targeting difficult in practice. The Tamil Nadu state government tried to identify woman-maintained households for the distribution of IRDP loans for economically active women. Using data from the 1981 census, and even with assistance from the Bureau of Economic Statistics and the District Statistics Officer, state officials were not able to distinguish female-maintained households from those headed by widows. Further, the widows who were identified were often not economically active and therefore did not fit the definition of the targeted population. The implementation of the National Perspective Plan faced similar problems, and government officials reported difficulty in identifying woman-headed households.

In contrast to the Chile case, where most of the errors appear to be of exclusion (of poor female heads who could not spare the time to apply or the foregone income to participate), the India experience analysed by Jain points to sizeable problems with the identification of female headship and with inclusions (leakages to non-poor people). It remains unclear how much of the Chilean success and Indian failure is due to inherent country-specific differences in the condition of female headship and how much of it is the result of different social infrastructures and political cultures surrounding targeting. In Chile, targeting programmes to the poor (mostly 'women-specific' nutrition and health interventions to pregnant women and to mothers and children) has been a fairly recent and non-controversial technocratic solution to economic and political problems posed by the recession starting in the late 1970s. This targeting has fully benefited from long-term government investments in physical and social infrastructures. In India, instead, the government has used targeting since independence for the much more controversial purpose of reserving a proportion or quota of public sector jobs to redress the historically social and economic discrimination of minority castes.

Jain's observations point to the need for more refined means to identify economically vulnerable woman-headed families for targeting than simply reported headship. They also illustrate the importance of effective monitoring, especially since in a resource-poor

developing economy such as India's, any poorly monitored development initiative may be appropriated by the more powerful. It may also
be the case, however, that targeting female headship for anti-poverty
reasons may be an appropriate strategy for Chile but not for India.
Decisions about targeting female headship should consider both the
costs and benefits of targeting and the context or environment in
which targeting takes place.

DISCUSSION

The experience with targeting woman-headed households is neither
rich enough nor well enough documented at this point to derive well-
grounded, useful recommendations for action. The cases of Chile and
India point in two directions – suggesting that targeting female heads
has not worked in India but may work effectively in Chile. A few
lessons can be drawn, however. First, these experiences support those
contained in several of the chapters in this volume, namely that
women participate actively in those initiatives which they recognise as
promoting their security and that of their families. From our two
country cases, it is clear that female heads are active participants in
public works, which reflect both their economic needs and the
economic benefits of low-wage schemes to female heads. Second, the
design of public works projects could be significantly improved to
increase the participation of poor female heads and reduce sex
discrimination in the wages paid. Third, improved measures of female
family headship and careful analyses of costs and benefits as well as of
the targeting environment can reduce screening errors and minimise
project costs.

Errors of exclusion in the Chile project could be minimised by,
among other things, extending the schedules for screening applicants
beyond regular work hours (adding some costs to the screening
process), and reducing costs of participation by providing cash
benefits to female heads to compensate for foregone income. Leakages
to the non-poor in India could be reduced by increasing investments
in the identification of female headship and in the monitoring of
targeted programmes to woman-headed families. Reported female
headship is a crude indicator of actual female headship. A more refined
indicator of female family maintenance would take into account
marital status of the head (to gauge origins) and presence and ages
of dependants. In addition, attempts could be made to identify sub-
families headed by women within male-headed households.

Governments that wish to implement anti-poverty programmes with constrained budgets should seriously consider targeting female headship as an innovative and potentially cost-effective policy option with spillover benefits to children. But they should exercise caution in design and implementation.

There can be sizeable direct and indirect benefits to participating families and to society from targeting poor woman-headed families. Female headship and poverty are strongly correlated in developing countries, and targeting female headship can reduce the poverty of women with larger benefits to children than those that would be obtained from targeting male-headed families with the same amount of resources. But there can also be potentially high costs which need to be anticipated and reduced. The costs to the agency that finances targeting female headship are administrative and political. Leakages to male-headed households and to non-poor female-headed households can be reduced by using a set of indicators beyond reported headship to identify female family headship; devising and implementing gender-informed public works and other self-targeted interventions designed to attract female participants; and delivering female-specific public goods. But the evidence shows that poor female heads also need services, jobs and cash transfers that are not female-specific. Targeting these benefits may antagonise the more powerful male constituency, so such programmes should anticipate and guard against potentially high political costs.

Policymakers in developing countries need not be too concerned about increasing the prevalence of female headship by creating perverse incentives influencing family formation and dissolution. Programmes should, however, anticipate increases in the prevalence of female-headed households as a result of changes in the living arrangements of female family heads who, as a result of the intervention, become able to afford independent housing. Programmes can quantify these predictable increases to minimise potential political backlash. Governments can, therefore, design interventions that anticipate and reduce administrative and political costs, making it increasingly attractive to target female headship. The next step for both governments and donor agencies is the willingness to invest more in experimental anti-poverty interventions that target female headship (including public initiatives to promote the economic responsibility attached to fatherhood) and in sound evaluations of the experiences of both NGOs and governments in this area.

NOTE

A revised version of this chapter will appear in *Economic Development and Cultural Change* (forthcoming).

REFERENCES

Acharya, S. and Panwalkar, V. G. (1988) *The Maharashtra Employment Guarantee Scheme: Impacts on Male and Female Labour*, Bangkok: The Population Council, Regional Office for South and East Asia.

Berheide, C. W. and Segal, M. T. (1989) 'Locating Women in the Development Process: Female Small-Holders in Malawi'. Paper presented at the National Women's Studies Association Meetings, June.

Besley, T. and Kanbur, R. (1990) 'The Principles of Targeting', Working papers 385, Washington, DC: World Bank.

Buvinić, M. and Mellencamp, A. (1983) 'Research on and by Women in Chile'. Report prepared for the Inter-American Foundation, July.

Buvinić, M., Youssef, N. and von Elm, B. (1978) 'Women-Headed Households: The Ignored Factor in Development Planning', Washington, DC: International Centre for Research on Women.

Buvinić, M., Valenzuela, J. P., Molina, T. and Gonzalez, E. (1992) 'The Fortunes of Adolescent Mothers and Their Children: A Case Study on the Transmission of Poverty in Santiago, Chile', *Population and Development Review* 18, 2, June: 269–297.

Chant, S. (1985) 'Single-Parent Families: Choice or Constraint? The Formation of Female-Headed Households in Mexican Shanty Towns', *Development and Change* 16: 635–656.

Chernichowsky, D. and Smith, C. (1979) 'Primary School Enrolment and Attendance in Rural Botswana', mimeograph, Washington, DC: World Bank.

Chipande, G. H. R. (1987) 'Innovation Adoption among Female-Headed Households: The Case of Malawi', *Development and Change* 18: 315–327.

DeGraff, D. S. and Bilsborrow, R. E. (1993) 'Female Headed Households and Family Welfare in Rural Ecuador', *Journal of Population Economics* 6, 4: 317–336.

Deolalikar, A. B. and Gaiha, R. (1992) 'Targeting of Rural Public Works: Are Women Less Likely to Participate?' Paper presented at the International Food Policy Research Institute Workshop on 'Intra-household Resource Allocation: Policy Issues and Research Methods', Washington, DC, 12–14 February.

Engle, P. (1991) 'Maternal Work and Child-Care Strategies in Peri-Urban Guatemala', *Child Development* 62: 954–965.

—— (1993) 'Influences of Mother's and Father's Income on Children's Nutritional Status in Guatemala', *Social Science and Medicine* 37, 11: 1,303–1,312.

Folbre, N. (1991) 'Mothers on Their Own: Policy Issues for Developing Countries'. Paper prepared for the joint ICRW/Population Council series on 'The Determinants and Consequences of Female-Headed Households'.

Fuchs, V. R. (1989) 'Women's Quest for Economic Equality', *Journal of Economic Perspectives* 3, 1: 25–41.

Garcia, M. (1991) 'Income Sources of the Malnourished Rural Poor in the Provinces of Abra Antique, and South Cotabato in the Philippines', working paper, Washington, DC: International Food Policy Research Institute (IFPRI).

Garfinkel, I. and McLanahan, S. S. (1986) *Single Mothers and Their Children*, Washington, DC: The Urban Institute Press.

Gulati, L. (1983) 'Impacts of Male Migration to the Middle East on the Family: Some Evidence from Kerala', working paper 76, India: Centre for Development Studies.

Jain, D. (1989) 'Women and Their Households – The Importance of Women in Macro Policies'. Presentation at joint ICRW/Population Council Seminar III: 'Determinants of Households Headed or Maintained by Women: Considerations of the Life-cycle', New York, 10–11 April.

——(1992) 'Experience of Targeting Women in India'. Paper prepared for joint Population Council/ICRW project on Female Headship and Poverty.

Jazairy, I., Alamgir, M. and Panuccio, T. (1992) *The State of World Rural Poverty*, New York: published for IFAD by New York University Press.

Johnson, C. and Rogers, B. Lorge (1993) 'Children's Nutritional Status in Female-Headed Households in the Dominican Republic', *Social Science and Medicine* 37, 11: 1,293–1,301.

Kazi, S. and Raza, B. (1989) 'Households Headed by Women: Income, Employment and Household Organisation'. Paper presented at the Fifth Annual General Meeting of the Pakistan Institute of Development Economics, Islamabad, 4–6 January.

Kennedy, E. (1992) 'Effects of Gender of Head of Household on Women's and Children's Nutritional Status'. Paper presented at the Workshop on The Effects of Policies and Programmes on Women, 16 January.

Kossoudji, S. and Mueller, E. (1983) 'The Economic and Demographic Status of Female-Headed Households in Rural Botswana', *Economic Development and Cultural Change* 31 (July): 831–859.

Krishnaswamy, K. S. and Rajagopal, S. (1985) 'Women in Employment: A Micro Study in Karnataka', in D. Jain and N. Banerjee (eds) *Tyranny of the Household*, New Delhi: Shakti Books.

Kumar, S. K. (1991) 'Income Sources of the Malnourished Poor in Rural Zambia', working paper, Washington, DC: International Food Policy Research Institute.

Kumari, R. (1989) *Women-Headed Households in Rural India*, New Delhi: Radiant Publishers.

Lastarria-Cornheil, S. (1988) 'Female Farmers and Agricultural Production in El Salvador', *Development and Change* 19: 585–615.

Levison, D. (1989) 'Family Composition and Child Labour: Survival Strategies of the Brazilian Poor'. Paper presented at the annual meeting of the Population Association of America, 30 March –1 April.

Louat, F., Grosh, M. E. and van der Gaag, J. (1992) 'Welfare Implications for Female Headship in Jamaican Households'. Paper presented at the International Food Policy Research Institute Workshop on 'Inter-

household Resource Allocation: Policy Issues and Research Methods',
Washington, DC, 12–14 February.

Merrick, T. W. and Schmink, M. (1983) 'Households Headed by Women and
Urban Poverty in Brazil', in M. Buvinić, M. Lycette and W. McGreevey
(eds) *Women and Poverty in the Third World*, Baltimore: Johns Hopkins
University Press.

Paes de Barros, R., Fox, L. and Pinto de Mendonca (1993) 'Female Headed
Households: Poverty and the Welfare of Children and Youths in Brazil'.
Paper presented for the joint ICRW/Population Council Programme on
Female Headship and Poverty in Developing Countries.

Ravallion, M. (1991) 'Reaching the Rural Poor Through Public Employment', *World Bank Research Observer* 6, 2: 153–175.

Rosenhouse, S. (1988) 'Identifying the Poor: Is Headship a Useful Concept?'
Paper prepared for joint ICRW/Population Council Seminar I: 'Concepts
and Classifications of Female-Headed Households: Implications and
Applications for National Statistics', New York, 12–13 December.

Schkolnik, M. (1991) 'Chile: Impacto del Gasto Social en los Hogares con
Jefatura Feminina'. Draft PREALC working paper, Santiago: PREALC.

Schwede, L. (1991) 'Family Strategies of Labor Allocation and Decision-
Making in a Matrilineal Islamic Society: The Minangkabau of West
Sumatra, Indonesia'. Unpublished Ph.D. dissertation, Cornell University.

Thomas, D. (1990) 'Intra-Household Resource Allocation: An Inferential
Approach', *The Journal of Human Resources* 25, 4: 635–664.

Tienda, M. and Ortega Salazar, S. (1980) *Female-Headed Households and
Extended Family Formations in Rural and Urban Peru*, Madison: Centre for
Demography and Ecology, University of Wisconsin.

Valenzuela, J. P. (1994) 'Caracteristicas de Pobreza de las Participantes en el
Plano Piloto para Jefas de Hogar', in M. E. Valenzuela, S. Venegas and C.
Andrade (eds) *De Mujer Sola a Jefa de Hogar: Genero, Pobreza y Politicas
Publicas*, Santiago: Servicio Nacional de la Mujer.

Valenzuela, M. E. (1992) 'Combinando la lucha contra la Pobreza y la
Discriminación de Género: Programmeas de Apoyo a Mujero Jefas de
Hogar de Escosos Recursos'. Paper prepared for the joint Population
Council/ICRW project on Female Headship and Poverty.

Vial, I., Muchnik, E. and Kain, J. (1988) 'Evaluation of Chile's Main
Nutrition Intervention Programme', mimeograph, Santiago: University
of Chile and Catholic University.

Wood, C. H. (1989) 'Women-headed Households and Child Mortality in
Brazil, 1960–1980'. Draft presented at joint ICRW/Population Council
Seminar II: 'Consequences of Female Headship and Female Maintenance',
Washington, DC, 27–28 February.

World Bank (1990) *World Development Report 1990: Poverty*, New York:
Oxford University Press.

INDEX

abortion 97, 99
Acharya, S. 143
Adamik, M. 7, 98, 103–5
Africa: cooperatives 52–3; credit associations 51–2; informal social security 51–3; peasant organisations 51, 52, 54–5, 56–7; social movements 53–6; structural adjustment programmes 45–9, 63–4; traditional social security 49–50; willingness to pay for healthcare 85; woman-headed households 47, 136, 137; women's professional associations 54
Afshar, H. 4
Aids 20, 87, 90
Alamgir, M. 132
Alma Ata conference (1978) 76–7
Amnesty International 14
Anheier, H.K. 61
Antigua 26
Antrobus, P. 35, 39, 41
armed conflict 2, 11–13; effect on social policy 12–13; rape 13–14

Balbo, L. 105
Bamako Initiative 83–4
Barbados Women's Forum 37, 40
Barnett, A. 20
Basu, A.M. 85
Basu, K. 85
Beall, J. 7, 69, 71

Belize Organisation for Women and Development (BOWAND) 36
Belize Rural Women's Association 36
Benda-Beckmann, F. von 49
Bennholdt-Thomsen, V. 47
Berger, P.L. 59–60
Berheide, C.W. 135, 136
Besley, T. 140
Bicego, G. 22
bilharzia 88
Bilsborrow, R.E. 138
Blaikie, P. 20
Bloom, G.H. 83
Bolivia: emergency social fund 143; family planning programmes 16–17
Bosnia 14
Botswana 135
Brazil: children's nutrition 137; targeting female headship 139; woman-headed households 135
Brown, A. 25–6
Bruchhaus, E.M. 49
Burgess, R. 1
Burkina Faso 54
Buvinić, M. 3, 8, 64, 137–9, 141, 143

Cameroon: co-financing programme of primary healthcare 55; credit associations 52; emergency funds 55;

Folbre, N. 133, 135
Foo, G.H.C. 121
food security 51; Senegal 56–7
food support: Jamaica 30; woman-
  headed households 139–40
Forsberg, B.C. 85
Fox, L. 138
French, J. 42, 43
Frey-Nakonz, R. 58
Fuchs, V.R. 138

Gaiha, R. 144
Garcia, M. 137
Garfinkel, I. 141, 147
Genberg, H. 72, 85
Getubig, I.P. 52
Ghai, D. 3
Gladwin, C.H. 46
Glagow, M. 61
global change 10–21
global insecurity: gender policies
  10–11; and social policy 11–15
  (see also social policy)
GOBI (growth monitoring, ORT,
  breastfeeding and
  immunisations) 83
GOBI/FFF (GOBI/family
  planning, food production and
  female literacy) 83
Goetz, A.M. 4
Grant, R. 10
Grenada 26
Grosh, M.E. 138
Grown, C. 89
Gsänger, H. 52, 59
Gulati, L. 135, 138
Guyana: Council on the Affairs and
  Status of Women (CAS-WIG)
  35; devaluation 31; Economic
  Recovery Programme 30–1; Red
  Thread Women's Development
  Project 36; retreat of state 30–1;
  social policy in 60s and 70s 25–
  6; structural adjustment
  programmes 30–1; water
  supplies 30–1, 38–9

Haddad, L. 47, 59
Hardiman, M. 73

Harriss, J. 80, 85
harvest insurance 55, 57
health services/policies:
  empowerment of women 89–91;
  evolution 71–2; future planning
  86–91; gender critique 74–5;
  gender perspective 67–8; health
  delivery planning 88–9; human
  development approach 86–7;
  impact on women of SAPs/state
  retreat 37–8; industrial nations
  models 73–4; informal security
  50; Jamaica 29, 38; maternal
  and child health (MCH) 68, 76,
  79–80, 83–4, 87; NGO systems
  55; policies 67–92; and poverty
  alleviation /8; primary
  healthcare programmes see
  primary healthcare; process 70–
  71; redistribution legacy 75–81;
  targeting 83–6; trends 69;
  Trinidad and Tobago 38;
  vulnerability 72
Henry, R. 25
Hernes, M.H. 105
HIV/Aids 20, 87, 90
human development 86–7
Hungary 96–103; changes in social
  policy 99–103; Gypsy
  households 100; old social policy
  98–9; Social Act 97, 101; social
  assistance system 97; Social
  Security Fund 99, 100;
  Unemployment Fund 100;
  Women's Association 97;
  women's employment 99–100,
  102
Hyden, G. 62–3

immunisation programmes 74, 75,
  79
INADES 51
income-generating projects 46
income-reducing strategies 39–40
India: Integrated Rural
  Development Programme
  (IRDP) 148–50; Maharashtra
  Employment Guarantee Scheme
  (EGS) 143, 144; National

UNICEF 37, 76; Bamako Initiative 83–4
United Kingdom: health policies 69; Overseas Development Administration 17–18
United Nations 12; Decade for Women (1975–85) 35, 77; Economic Commission for Latin America and the Caribbean (UN/ECLAC) 35; First UN Development Decade (1960–69) 75; International Women's Year 35
user charges 84–6

Valenzuela, J P 145, 147
van der Gaag, J. 138
Vial, I. 138, 147
village health workers 80–1
violence 88
von Elm, B. 141
von Werlhof, C. 47

wage levels: Guyana 31; Jamaica 29–30; Trinidad and Tobago 32
Walker, A. 25, 27
WAND 37, 40, 41
war see armed conflict
water supplies 88; Guyana 30–1, 38–9
Welbourn, A. 85
West Africa see Africa

Whitehead, A. 71
Wilkens, W. 49
woman-headed households 132–51; children's nutrition 137–8; Chile 136, 140; dependency burden 135; education 138–9; gender-related economic gap 135; India 135; Latin America 134, 136, 137; poverty 134–9; West Africa 47, 136, 137
woman-maintained families 132–51
women: and global insecurity 10–11; instrumental use of 15–19; professional associations 54; and social welfare 3–5
Women in Development (WID) policies 64, 71, 77–8
Wood, C.H. 137
World Bank: Bolivia 16–17; Caribbean 27; Jamaica 29; Malaysia 107, 110, 112
World Health Organisation 76
Wuyts, M. 69

Young, K. 36, 71
Youssef, N. 141

Zambia: children's nutrition 137; willingness to pay for healthcare 85–6
Zimbabwe 18